LIFE Quest

Volume One

Authors
Sharon R. Berry, Ph.D.
Ollie E. Gibbs, Ed.D.

Published by LifeWay Christian School Resources
© 2000 Christian Academic Publications and Services, Inc.
Revised 2006
Reprinted 2009, 2010

Created and Developed by
Christian Academic Publications and Services, Inc.
Birmingham, Alabama

ISBN: 978-1-4158-3149-6
Item 005035097

Dewey Decimal Classification: 248.82
Subject Heading: CHRISTIAN LIFE/TEENAGERS/JESUS CHRIST—TEACHINGS

Printed in the United States of America

Student Ministry Publishing
LifeWay Church Resources
One LifeWay Plaza
Nashville, TN   37234-0174

For ordering or inquiries visit *www.lifeway.com* or write LifeWay Church Resource Customer Service, One LifeWay Plaza, Nashville, TN 37234-0113.

TABLE OF CONTENTS

Christmas reminds you of Jesus' birth. Easter commemorates His death and resurrection. What happened before, between, during, and after these events is the topic of your study in the course *LifeQuest*, a study of the life of Christ. Each week you will read Scriptures, focus on the works and words of Jesus Christ, then make personal application to your own life. It's a challenging but fun course with lots of activities.

You will share the course with a group of friends who are facing similar issues in life as they communicate through instant messages. Here are their names and a little information about them.

 IM4Him: Sarah, a high-school freshman, has three special school friends. They often correspond by instant messages. Sarah is a serious student who has a great relationship with her older sister.

 2B4Givn: Ginny is Sarah's older sister. She graduated from the same Christian school that Sarah and the others attend. Ginny is a sophomore attending college away from home.

 QTee: Megan is Sarah's best friend. Megan is fun-loving and sometimes speaks before thinking, which can cause problems at home and with her friends. She enjoys playing golf.

 PHETI: Tyler, whose last name is Fisher, chose his IM name because it is the phonetic equivalent for fish (Ph = f, E = i; TI = sh). Tyler also likes fishing, especially deep-sea fishing with his dad.

 Gr8-1: Tim's IM name displays his sense of self-confidence—except about his height and athletic ability. His goal in life is to someday become a medical missionary.

 UthPstr: Pastor Scott is Youth Pastor at Sarah's church. She has invited all the students to her church, so they know him well. They respect his judgment and include him in several discussions.

Studying the life of Christ without consideration for your own life would be a waste of time and effort. Knowledge alone is for naught. If you have ever wondered . . .

> "Is God really there?"
>
> "Is Jesus really God's Son?"
>
> "Will believing this make any difference in my life?"

. . . this is the year to find the answers to your questions. Begin with the simple prayer, "God, show me yourself and Your Son. If You are really there, I want to know."

The possibilities are endless as you determine to conscientiously take ownership over what you learn during the year. More than what your instructor demands, the real value of this course will be what you put into it and get out of it. That all depends on you—will you commit to letting the Lord speak to you from the pages of Scripture?

The Apostle John was the author of the Gospel that bears his name. He tells us that if all the things Jesus did ". . . were written one by one, I suppose that even the world itself could not contain the books that would be written." Therefore, John, along with other authors, selected carefully the details of Christ's life to be ". . . written that you may believe that Jesus is the Christ, the Son of God, and that believing you may have life in His name."

That you may believe and have life in His name—that is the purpose of your study as you embark on *LifeQuest*. May you be blessed as you consider week by week the wonderful words and works of our Lord Jesus Christ.

–The Authors

STUDY HIS LIFE   FIND DIRECTION   KNOW HIM   HAVE A RIGHT ATTITUDE
BECOME CHRIST-LIKE   KNOW GOD'S WORD   SEARCH FOR ANSWERS
MAKE MATURE CHOICES   COMMIT MYSELF   HAVE GOOD RELATIONSHIPS
STUDY HIS LIFE   FIND DIRECTION   KNOW HIM   HAVE A RIGHT ATTITUDE
BECOME CHRIST-LIKE   KNOW GOD'S WORD   SEARCH FOR ANSWERS
MAKE MATURE CHOICES   COMMIT MYSELF   HAVE GOOD RELATIONSHIPS
STUDY HIS LIFE   FIND DIRECTION   KNOW HIM   HAVE A RIGHT ATTITUDE
BECOME CHRIST-LIKE   KNOW GOD'S WORD   SEARCH FOR ANSWERS
MAKE MATURE CHOICES   COMMIT MYSELF   HAVE GOOD RELATIONSHIPS
STUDY HIS LIFE   FIND DIRECTION   KNOW HIM   HAVE A RIGHT ATTITUDE
BECOME CHRIST-LIKE   KNOW GOD'S WORD   SEARCH FOR ANSWERS
MAKE MATURE CHOICES   COMMIT MYSELF   HAVE GOOD RELATIONSHIPS
STUDY HIS LIFE   FIND DIRECTION   KNOW HIM   HAVE A RIGHT ATTITUDE
BECOME CHRIST-LIKE   KNOW GOD'S WORD   SEARCH FOR ANSWERS
MAKE MATURE CHOICES   COMMIT MYSELF   HAVE GOOD RELATIONSHIPS
STUDY HIS LIFE   FIND DIRECTION   KNOW HIM   HAVE A RIGHT ATTITUDE
BECOME CHRIST-LIKE   KNOW GOD'S WORD   SEARCH FOR ANSWERS
MAKE MATURE CHOICES   COMMIT MYSELF   HAVE GOOD RELATIONSHIPS
STUDY HIS LIFE   FIND DIRECTION   KNOW HIM   HAVE A RIGHT ATTITUDE
BECOME CHRIST-LIKE   KNOW GOD'S WORD   SEARCH FOR ANSWERS
MAKE MATURE CHOICES   COMMIT MYSELF   HAVE GOOD RELATIONSHIPS
STUDY HIS LIFE   FIND DIRECTION   KNOW HIM   HAVE A RIGHT ATTITUDE
BECOME CHRIST-LIKE   KNOW GOD'S WORD   SEARCH FOR ANSWERS
MAKE MATURE CHOICES   COMMIT MYSELF   HAVE GOOD RELATIONSHIPS
STUDY HIS LIFE   FIND DIRECTION   KNOW HIM   HAVE A RIGHT ATTITUDE
BECOME CHRIST-LIKE   KNOW GOD'S WORD   SEARCH FOR ANSWERS
MAKE MATURE CHOICES   COMMIT MYSELF   HAVE GOOD RELATIONSHIPS

THE LIFE OF CHRIST

QUESTTRUTH

Jesus Christ is God's Son. As a member of the Trinity, He is both distinct from and unified with God the Father, and God the Holy Spirit, into the One Triune God. Thus, He existed before time began.

 IM4Him: This has been a really long day! You know I've been excited about my first day. I certainly wasn't disappointed! But I can't believe all the homework. I know I was only in the 5th grade when you were in high school. I just don't remember that you brought so much work home on your first day. Did you?

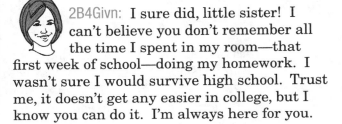 2B4Givn: I sure did, little sister! I can't believe you don't remember all the time I spent in my room—that first week of school—doing my homework. I wasn't sure I would survive high school. Trust me, it doesn't get any easier in college, but I know you can do it. I'm always here for you.

 IM4Him: Thanks! I'm fine with tonight's assignment, but I do have something that's been bothering me lately. Matter of fact, it's kind of bothered me all summer.

 2B4Givn: What's that? You didn't say anything while I was home this summer. Are you sick? Is everything okay at school?

 IM4Him: Everything is great at school, and I'm not sick. I've just been thinking a lot about God. I know I'm a Christian, and I'm not afraid of dying or anything. I don't know why God is on my mind so much right now. I really want to have a better understanding of who He is.

 2B4Givn: I'm glad everything's okay. But I'm a little confused about what's bothering you. Can you be more specific?

 IM4Him: Sorry if I'm not making a lot of sense. I'm not even sure how to ask the questions. Who is God anyway? I'm just confused about who He really is.

2B4Givn: Don't apologize. A lot of people find it hard to ask questions about God. Maybe I can help since I've been teaching this subject in my dorm Bible study. Wait and I'll click in my notes.

2B4Givn: The Greeks were worried that they might forget a god. In their desire not to offend a god who didn't have his or her own altar, they made sure that at least one altar was set aside for any "unknown god."

Paul used the opportunity to teach the Athenians who God really is. Take a look at verses 24-31. In these verses, Paul outlined eight basic facts about God. What are they?

IM4Him: Let's see . . .

- God is the Creator of all things.
- God is Lord of heaven.
- God gives life and breath to all things.
- God is in control of everything that happens in the world.
- God is living and personal, not a carved image.
- God is our Father and desires a relationship with us.
- God requires repentance for our sins.
- God will one day judge the entire world in righteousness.

2B4Givn: Good job! You see, just like the Athenians, people have a very confused understanding of who God is. If you were to go up to strangers and ask them to describe God, you would probably be very surprised at the unusual responses that you would receive. Here's some more of my notes.

FILE SHARING

5. Unless we have a correct understanding of who God is, it is impossible for us to worship Him as we should. That's why we have the first of the Ten Commandments: "I am the Lord your God. . . . You shall have no other gods before Me" (Exodus 20:2–3).

6. Reminder: Our tendency is to create God in our own image. We expect God to have the same abilities, priorities, likes, and dislikes that we have. But God is not like that. He is not going to say that everything we do and think is okay with Him. We are commanded to know Him as He really is. That's why Paul set the record straight on Mars Hill by pointing out these eight key facts about who God is.

7. It's a lot like when we first began dressing ourselves. Remember how much trouble it was to button a coat? We never could get the first button in the right hole. Then, of course, if the first button was buttoned wrong, the rest of the buttons were wrong.

8. Paul wanted the citizens of Athens to have their facts right about who God is. If they started out wrong by worshiping a god made of silver or gold, then for all of life they would be living a lie. Their sacrifices, devotions and prayers would be meaningless. If they were not worshiping the real God, their worship would be in vain.

IM4Him: People do like to define God according to their own imagination. I remember Mr. Gifford saying that the limits of our human minds make it impossible to understand how magnificent and powerful God is. Therefore, any product of our imagination is far inferior to the true nature of God.

 2B4Givn: I agree totally. Let's look again at the eight facts about God that you found in Acts 17:24-31. Pay close attention to the first and last facts.

FILE SHARING

9. Paul began by declaring that God was the Creator of everything and the Lord of heaven. He ended his sermon by announcing that one day God would judge the entire world. These two facts were especially important.

10. Note how Paul made his argument. The God he described was not made by the hands of men, but had been in existence before the world was even formed. More importantly, this same God would bring judgment unless people repented of their sins.

11. Paul's message to the Athenians was more than a Bible lesson on who God is. Paul was laying the foundation for a future time when he would explain to them the relationship between God and His Son, Jesus Christ.

12. The Bible is the historical record of God's plan of redemption. Jesus Christ, God's Son, is the Messiah promised in the Old Testament. Only through Him could people be saved. That's why all time dates from Jesus' birth; B.C. means "before Christ"; A.D. means Anno Domini, "in the year of our Lord." Jesus is the central point of human history.

13. This relationship between God and His Son was clearly explained by John—"And we know that the Son of God has come and has given us an understanding, that we may know Him who is true; and we are in Him who is true, in His Son Jesus Christ. This is the true God and eternal life" (1 John 5:20).

14. The same facts that are true about God are also true about His Son Jesus Christ. Jesus Christ was "in the beginning" (John 1:1,3,10,14) and will one day come to judge the whole world (John 5:22). The Bible repeatedly testifies to the truthfulness of Jesus' statement, "I and My Father are one" (John 10:30).

IM4Him: Does that mean we can better understand who God is if we know who Jesus is? Seems like I remember a verse that states Jesus is the exact image of God.

2B4Givn: That's right! For a moment, go back in time and imagine what it would have been like to walk along the seashore with Jesus and His disciples. All of a sudden Jesus stops, looks at you, and asks, "Who am I to you?" Maybe, like the disciples, you'd be stuck for an answer. I wrote my thoughts in my notes.

FILE SHARING

15. Who is Jesus? You're not quite sure what to say. You know that some people think He's a nut, while others are convinced He's a troublemaker. When Jesus asked Peter the same question, Peter acted as if he was reporting the latest Gallup poll: "Thirty-one percent think You're Elijah, 43 percent think You're John the Baptist, and another 26 percent think You're one of the prophets."

16. Of course, the Biblical answer is: "You're the Son of God, the second person of the Trinity, the Lord of all creation, the Savior of the world." But, as you continue to stand there, you realize that Jesus is not interested in the kind of response you would give on a Bible test. He wants to know who He is to you, personally and intimately.

17. Although He is the Lord of all creation and the Savior of the world, He wants a personal relationship with you. He wants you to know that you never have to be lonely again. He wants you to know that He is ready to forgive you for your sins. He wants you to know that He will show you where you fit in this world. He wants to guide your decisions about your family and your future.

18. For the rest of your life, in one form or another, people will be seeking an answer to the question, "Who is God?" In their quest for the truth, many will make the same mistake as the Athenians. They will exchange the truth of God for a lie and serve created things rather than the Creator (Romans 1:25). That doesn't necessarily mean that your friends or neighbors will worship images or idols. But it does mean that they will try to fashion a "god" who thinks and acts like they do, something very different from the true God in heaven.

IM4Him: So, what you're saying is that if we truly understand who God is, we won't try to make Him into someone who always agrees with what we think and does what we want done.

2B4Givn: You're exactly right! If we try to make God in our own image, we reduce Him to our own level. The Bible makes it very clear that He is the Creator, Lord of Lords, and Savior of the world. Remember, Jesus said, "I and my Father are one." As we learn more about Jesus, we will better understand who God is.

IM4Him: Thanks for taking the time tonight. It's late, and I still have a lot of homework to do. We'll talk more about this later.

QUESTFILE 1.1

John 1:1-5,9-14 Complete your notes based on class discussion.

Phrases	Related Verses	Notes
In the beginning	Genesis 1:1	
was the Word,	1 John 1:1-2	
and the Word was with God,	John 17:1-5	
and the Word was God.	1 John 5:7	

Phrases	Related Verses	Notes
All things were made through Him,	Colossians 1:16-17	
In Him was life,	1 John 5:11	
But as many as received Him, to them He gave the right to become children of God,	John 3:36	
And the Word became flesh and dwelt among us,	Colossians 1:21-23	

QuestFile 1.2

The Nature of God Fill in your notes.

1

Attribute

**Self-existent
A living being
Complete
     within Himself**

Scripture

*Isaiah 40;
Exodus 3:14;
John 8:24,28;
Romans 1:20; 2:15;
3:19,24-25*

What it means _____
_____
_____
_____
_____

Why it is important to me _____
_____
_____

2

Attribute

**Eternal
Infinite
Everlasting**

Scripture

*Isaiah 40:6-8,26,28;
Psalm 90:2*

What it means _____
_____
_____
_____
_____

Why it is important to me _____
_____
_____

3

Attribute

**Unchanging
Immutable**

Scripture

*Isaiah 40:28;
James 1:17;
Malachi 3:6*

What it means _____
_____
_____
_____
_____

Why it is important to me _____
_____
_____

4	**All-powerful Omnipotent Sovereign authority**	**What it means** _____ _____ _____ _____ _____
Attribute		
Scripture	*Isaiah 40:10-12, 15-24; Psalm 103:19; 111:6–9; Isaiah 14:24-27*	**Why it is important to me** _____ _____ _____ _____

5	**All-knowing Omniscient**	**What it means** _____ _____ _____ _____ _____
Attribute		
Scripture	*Isaiah 40:13-14, 27-28; Psalm 44:21; 1 Samuel 16:7; Proverbs 2:6-7*	**Why it is important to me** _____ _____ _____ _____

6	**Everywhere at the same time Omnipresent**	**What it means** _____ _____ _____ _____ _____
Attribute		
Scripture	*Isaiah 40:5; Psalm 139:4-12; Jeremiah 23:23-24*	**Why it is important to me** _____ _____ _____ _____

7	Holy Impeccable Without sin	What it means _____ _____ _____ _____ _____
Attribute		
Scripture	*Isaiah 40:25; Isaiah 6:3; Leviticus 11:44-45*	Why it is important to me _____ _____ _____

8	Creator Maker of all	What it means _____ _____ _____ _____
Attribute		
Scripture	*Isaiah 40:2,12, 25-26; Genesis 1:1; Psalm 19:1-2; 24:1-2; Jeremiah 51:15-16*	Why it is important to me _____ _____ _____

9	Loving Merciful Caring	What it means _____ _____ _____ _____
Attribute		
Scripture	*Isaiah 40:1-2,9,11, 29-31; Psalm 63:3; Jeremiah 31:3; John 3:16; Exodus 34:5-14; Psalm 84:2-3,10*	Why it is important to me _____ _____ _____

Family Chatroom   Interact with your parents or another adult and record their responses.

1. Do you believe in God? Why? _____

_____

_____

_____

2. Do you believe Jesus Christ is God? Why? _____

_____

_____

_____

3. What does "Trinity" mean in relation to God? _____

_____

_____

_____

4. It's been said that even if Jesus were not God, He is the most influential person to have ever lived. Name three reasons why this is true.

_____

_____

_____

_____

_____

_____
Parent's Signature

THE OLD AND THE NEW

QUESTTRUTH

The Bible presents the plan of God to bring redemption to mankind—its need, its nation, its Person, its explanation and its end. Jesus Christ is the promised Messiah sent to Earth to complete God's plan.

 IM4Him: I have an impossible assignment!! I've got to explain the plan of redemption using only the Old Testament.

 2B4Givn: I remember those Bible classes—and the tough assignments. I'll be glad to help.

 IM4Him: Can my friend, Tyler Fisher, join our conversation? He sits next to me in class. Neither of us knows how to do this assignment.

 2B4Givn: No problem—the more the merrier. You'll do lots of homework in the next several years. Many times you'll probably ask yourself, *Why is this stuff important?*

 IM4Him: That's exactly how I feel about this assignment. It's been almost half an hour, and we still don't know how to start.

 2B4Givn: Actually, Mr. Gifford's assignment makes a lot of sense. Suppose you were trying to talk with a Jewish person about salvation. Since the Jewish people do not accept the New Testament, how would you explain that Jesus Christ died for them?

 PHETI: I see your point. They only accept what's written in the Old Testament. Still, that's a lot of books. Where do we start?

2B4Givn: You have to focus on Old Testament prophecy. Do you realize that the vast majority of biblical prophecy concerns either the First Coming of Jesus Christ—which includes His ministry, death, resurrection, and ascension—or His Second Coming? Revelation 19:10 reminds us, "For the testimony of Jesus is the spirit of prophecy." The primary purpose of prophecy is to tell about Jesus.

PHETI: But we don't have time to study all of the Old Testament prophecies to find out which ones tell about Jesus. Our paper is due at the end of the week!

 2B4Givn: Relax! I've got a book that I think will help. Let me get back to you in a few minutes.

 2B4Givn: Hi, I'm back! I'm going to give you four sets of prophetic verses from the Old Testament to read. I want you to get back to me and tell me what these verses tell us about Jesus. Here are the verses.

- Prophecy 1—Genesis 49:10 and Isaiah 7:14
- Prophecy 2—Isaiah 61:1
- Prophecy 3—Psalm 41: 9 and Isaiah 53:3,5-6
- Prophecy 4—Psalm 16:10; 68:18

 PHETI: That's a lot to look up! Why don't you just tell us what they mean? We could write them down.

 2B4Givn: Hey guys, I'm not writing your paper for you! You two need to tell me what the prophecies are about. Then we'll discuss them.

 IM4Him: Okay, we're ready. Prophecy 1 tells us that God will send a Savior. Prophecy 2 tells us that this Savior is for everyone. Prophecy 3 tells us that He will be crucified. Prophecy 4 tells us that He will rise from the grave.

 2B4Givn: Very good—I'm impressed. You are beginning to understand that the Old Testament is the prophetic pathway that reveals Jesus, the coming Messiah, to us. It's through prophecy that we can share the plan of salvation from the Old Testament. That's the approach you want to take for this assignment. But wait! You'll also need to talk about why this stuff is important. Why is it important—to you personally—to know that Jesus is the fulfillment of Old Testament prophecy?

IM4Him: But that's not part of the assignment. I know, I know. . . . Why is it important to me to know that Jesus is the fulfillment of Old Testament prophecy?

2B4Givn: Let me explain it this way. Think about a piece of thread, perhaps one used to sew together pieces of clothing. It's often been said that Jesus Christ is the "Scarlet Thread" that ties together all of Scripture. The central theme or thread of the Bible is redemption. Because of Adam's sin, all have sinned (Romans 5:12). Beginning with Genesis 3:15, God describes the plan of redemption that He prepared to restore mankind to a right relationship with Him. God's plan calls for a Messiah, a Savior, who would become the perfect sacrifice for the sins of mankind.

Jesus Christ is the Savior that God sent. The story of His coming is the thread that ties together all of the books of the Old Testament. The thread is scarlet because it represents His blood. Right from the beginning, God required a blood sacrifice for the atonement of sins (Leviticus 17:11; Ephesians 1:7).

PHETI: Wow! Now I see how you can explain the plan of redemption from the Old Testament. The more we study the Bible, the more we see Jesus on every page.

2B4Givn: Still, you need to understand why this is important to you. Tyler, I know you watched the All-Star baseball game last July. Do you remember what the National League coach said after they won the game?

PHETI: Hmmm! During the post-game interview he said, "That's what it's all about!" What do you think he was talking about? What is "IT"?

2B4Givn: Substitute the word "LIFE" for the word "IT" and you will have your answer. The coach is saying that winning the All-Star game is what LIFE is all about. But we all know that LIFE is not just about winning baseball games. Take a look at the last page of an article I just read. I think it fits.

FILE SHARING

So, in your life right now, what is IT all about? What is the one thing that gives meaning to your life? Is IT being a part of the team, a special friend or your family? Is IT a person, hobby or having lots of money?

For centuries, people have searched for the one thing that would give meaning to life. Some have sought wealth and power. Others have defined life by doing good works. Unfortunately, too many have gone to their grave and never found the answer.

Libraries are filled with books describing man's answers to the great questions of life:

What is real?
What is good?

But it is Jesus who truly answers those questions in John 14:6 when He says, "I am the way, the truth, and the life." Jesus' response to all who have sought the meaning of life is to believe in Him.

Why is this so important? Because happiness, success, satisfaction, and peace cannot be found in winning games, having a lot of money or doing good works. We find out what IT—LIFE—is really all about when we accept Jesus Christ as our personal Savior.

PHETI: That sure fits with Mark 8:36-37, "For what will it profit a man if he gains the whole world, and loses his own soul? Or what will a man give in exchange for his soul?"

2B4Givn: Great, Tyler! Stating it a different way, Jesus asks, "What is most important to you?" That's a question we all need to think about.

IM4Him: We understand what you're saying. Thanks for taking so much time to help us tonight. We really appreciate you.

God's Eternal Plan Write four truths you remember about God's eternal plan.

The Bible Presents God's Plan of Redemption

Record your notes during class discussion.

The NEED Genesis, Chapters 1–11
(Genesis 3:15; Romans 5:12,17)

_____

_____

_____

_____

_____

The NATION Genesis 12 through Malachi
(Genesis 12:1-3; Galatians 3:8,14-15; Romans 4:3,20-25)

_____

_____

_____

_____

_____

The PERSON **The Gospels**
(Matthew 1:21; Luke 19:10)

_____

_____

_____

_____

_____

The EXPLANATION **Acts through Jude**
(Genesis 3:15; Romans 5:12,17)

_____

_____

_____

_____

_____

The END **Revelation**
(Revelation 5:9; 7:9; 21:1-3)

_____

_____

_____

_____

_____

QuestTruth

The Bible is the Word of God, divinely inspired and without error. Its central message is salvation through Jesus Christ, God's promised Messiah.

QTee: I've never had a project that was due in two different classes at the same time. How are you doing on your outline? Remember, it's due on Monday.

IM4Him: It's going okay. I've just never thought about how God has control over political leaders. I always knew that He had control over leaders in the Bible, like Nebuchadnezzar and Pontius Pilate. But it never occurred to me that God also had control over leaders like Winston Churchill, Adolf Hitler, and Joseph Stalin.

QTee: Did Mrs. Stewart ask you that strange question in your history class today: Is your life just an accident? She did in ours. It was really funny to listen to the reactions of others.

IM4Him: I wasn't in class today. I had to go to the dentist after lunch, so I don't know what you're talking about. It sounds interesting; tell me more.

QTee: She was talking about when some couples find out they are going to have a baby, and they say it was an accident. In other words, they weren't planning to have a baby. She then asked us to imagine being able to go back to start all over again. What would the odds be that your mother and father would once again produce you—exactly as you are today?

She quoted medical experts, who said that the chances for this happening exactly the same way again would be 1 out of 1,000,000,000,000,000. Her point was, we are not accidents! We did not JUST HAPPEN. Before we were ever conceived by our parents, we were already in the mind of God—just like it states in Psalm 139 and Ephesians 1.

IM4Him: Sounds like she was trying to make the connection between the assignment due in her class and the one in Bible class. What else did she say?

QTee: She made three points. Let me click in the list.

QTee: She also said that even back in the first century, the Apostle Paul reminded us that the birth of Jesus Christ occurred exactly according to God's plan. She read Galatians 4:4-5 to us—"But when the fullness of the time had come, God sent forth His Son, born of a woman, born under the law, to redeem those who were under the law, that we might receive the adoption as sons." The "fullness of the time" was Paul's way of saying "God's timetable."

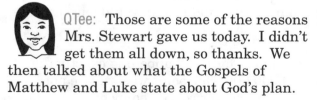

IM4Him: I really wish I hadn't missed class today. But I'm remembering a lesson Pastor Scott taught us. God chose the exact time in history for Jesus to come. Here are the six reasons he gave.

QTee: Those are some of the reasons Mrs. Stewart gave us today. I didn't get them all down, so thanks. We then talked about what the Gospels of Matthew and Luke state about God's plan.

IM4Him: Thanks for your help in filling in my notes. Let's start with Matthew first. I have my Bible if you need for me to look up some verses.

QTee: Okay, look at the first verse of Chapter 1. It states, "The book of the genealogy of Jesus Christ, the Son of David, the Son of Abraham." Mrs. Stewart said that Matthew began with the genealogy of Jesus to remind us that Jesus was a descendent of Abraham. By doing this, Matthew confirmed that Jesus Christ was the fulfillment of the promise made to Abraham in Genesis 12. She then wrote "Genesis 12:2-3" and "Romans 15:29" on the overhead.

> **FACTOID**
>
> Christ was born about 4 B.C., "before Christ." How can it be? The calendar used by the Romans had undergone several changes until the sixth century, when the adopted calendar still contained an error of five to six years—not a significant number when reconstructing dates from antiquity.

IM4Him: Wait a minute. Let me read. . . . Okay, looks like the two verses show us how Paul realized that Jesus Christ was the fulfillment of God's promise to Abraham in Genesis 12.

QTee: Right! Over the Genesis verses she wrote the words "God's Promise." Over the Romans verse she wrote the words "Fulfillment—Jesus Christ."

IM4Him: Okay, I got it! I also have a reference in my Bible to Galatians 3:16: "Now to Abraham and his Seed were the promises made. He does not say, 'And to seeds,' as of many, but as of one, 'And to your Seed,' who is Christ."

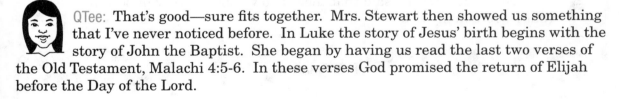

QTee: That's good—sure fits together. Mrs. Stewart then showed us something that I've never noticed before. In Luke the story of Jesus' birth begins with the story of John the Baptist. She began by having us read the last two verses of the Old Testament, Malachi 4:5-6. In these verses God promised the return of Elijah before the Day of the Lord.

IM4Him: Oh, I remember. The Day of the Lord refers to God's judgment, and not the birth of Christ. Still, John the Baptist came in the "spirit," or likeness, of Elijah when he preached for people to repent.

QTee: Right. But what's important is that the phrase "to turn the hearts of the fathers to the children" appears both in Malachi and in Luke 1:17. It seemed like the whole class was confused at that point. To help us understand, Mrs. Stewart wrote her explanation on the board. Here's what I wrote in my notes.

In Luke's gospel the boldness of John the Baptist is compared to the spirit and power of Elijah. Elijah not only foretold of a day of judgment (Day of the Lord), but also of a return of God's people to Him.

With the same boldness, John the Baptist would also preach a message of repentance, pleading for God's people to return to Him. At the same time, he would fulfill the prophecy of Isaiah 40:3 to "prepare the way of the Lord." The announcement of the birth of John the Baptist tied together the prophecies of Isaiah and Malachi.

IM4Him: Now I get it. God revealed His plan for both Jesus and John the Baptist hundreds of years before the events actually happened.

QTee: Hold on! There's more. Mrs. Stewart had us look for the similarity between Luke 1:32 and Matthew 1:1. Do you see what they have in common? Look—it's right there.

IM4Him: Luke's verse talks about the angel's announcement to Mary. Matthew 1:1 is the beginning of a genealogy. Wait! I get it! They both talk about the relationship of Jesus to David.

QTee: Yes! Mrs. Stewart said that these two verses are very important. Here's what I wrote in my notes.

Matthew describes Jesus as the Son of David. Luke reminds us that Jesus would be given David's throne. David's throne was an Old Testament symbol of the future rule of the Messiah (2 Samuel 7:13-16; Psalm 89:26-29).

Matthew and Luke were making sure that we understood the link between the Old Testament prophecies and the birth of Jesus Christ. Both Matthew and Luke wanted their readers to know that God's prophetic timeline had been fulfilled in Jesus Christ. They wanted to establish a clear, irrefutable link between the Old Testament promises and Jesus' birth.

IM4Him: It seems that the birth of Jesus Christ was the next step in God's plan of redemption. His birth was no accident, and it was no surprise to God. Now I understand why Mrs. Stewart asked if a person's life today was an accident. The births of both John the Baptist and Jesus were certainly not accidents. They were a part of God's plan. Stands to reason that each of us is also a part of His plan.

 QTee: It's an awesome thought but hard to really accept—especially on days when I feel so worthless. Anyway, let's finish the notes. Mrs. Stewart explained how the prophecy of the coming Messiah had been revealed throughout the Old Testament. She told us that for centuries the Israelites looked forward to the coming Messiah. Of course, they hoped He would come during their lifetime. But they obviously didn't know God's timetable.

 IM4Him: Now I'm starting to understand the connection between Bible and history for our project. Life is not an accident! Things don't just happen. Maybe we don't understand everything that's going on around us, but God does—and He is in complete control.

QTee: Yeah, it's just like Mrs. Stewart said—history is HIS STORY. Still, when so many bad things happen—wars, terrorism, hunger, AIDS—it's hard to understand that the world is really in His hands.

IM4Him: In Bible class today we talked about how the uncertainties of life can get you down. Mr. Gifford is right. We all face problems every day. I know some people who are really sick. Then there's Matt's family—his dad just lost his job. It was a total shock to their family.

QTee: That's what I mean. So many things happen that take us by surprise. But I guess these things aren't a surprise to God. That's the point Mrs. Stewart made in class. Just as the Israelites never lost hope that God had a plan, we shouldn't lose hope either. History will always unfold according to His plan. We just need to trust Him.

 IM4Him: Thanks for your encouragement, and double thanks for the notes from class. Why don't we get together over the weekend to work on our outlines. SYL!

The Gospels Take notes as the class overviews the four Gospels.

Matthew	Mark
About the author	
Why written	
Distinctives	
Presents Christ as	

	Luke	John
About the author		
Why written		
Distinctives		
Presents Christ as		

Family Chatroom/Every Child Is Special

Interact with your parents about the following questions.

1. Was there anything unique about expecting my birth, or about my infancy, that made you feel I was "ordained by God"?

_____

_____

_____

2. Do I have any abilities or personality traits that seem to make me unique and useful to God?

_____

_____

_____

3. What special plans or directions do you think God might have for my future?

_____

_____

_____

_____

_____

_____

_____

_____
Parent's Signature

REMINDER: If your teacher requested baby pictures, be sure to take them tomorrow.

QUESTFILE 3.3

Mark 8:35-37 Write your answer to the question: Do you think that life is an accident?

_____

_____

_____

_____

_____

_____

_____

_____

_____

_____

_____

_____

_____

_____

_____

_____

_____

_____

_____

_____

Things don't just happen. • God has a plan! • Things don't just happen. • God has a plan! • Things don't just happen.

Things don't just happen. • God has a plan! • Things don't just happen. • God has a plan! • Things don't just happen.

A CHILD IS BORN

QuestTruth

Jesus Christ was conceived of the Holy Spirit and born of the virgin Mary. As God incarnate, in the flesh, He was both perfect God and perfect man.

PHETI: Thanks for the invitation; I'd never been to your church before. Your youth pastor seems like a great guy. I really appreciated what he had to say tonight.

QTee: I agree with him that it's tough to feel nobody cares about what's going on in your life. We need to be more aware of what is happening to other people. Seems like we're always too focused on ourselves.

IM4Him: You mean like what's going on with Drew's family? His parents are getting a divorce, right? That's really sad. Have you guys talked with Drew or prayed for him and his family?

QTee: I haven't. So he's probably feeling just like our youth pastor said. He probably feels that nobody cares—not even God.

IM4Him: I liked the way Pastor Scott defined "perspective" tonight in his lesson. Perspective is "the ability to view things according to their true importance." He's right. God's perspective is very different from our perspective. Did anyone write down the Scripture reference he gave?

PHETI: It's 1 Samuel 16:7, "For the Lord does not see as man sees; for man looks at the outward appearance, but the Lord looks at the heart." He sure made his point that people are more concerned with how things look than what they are really like. The beautiful wrapping paper and bow on a gift are not at all as important as what is inside the box.

QTee: I agree. Just like he said, the banana tastes a whole lot better than the peel; and when you're thirsty, it's the soft drink inside—not the shape of the bottle—that you really want.

FACTOID

The land of Palestine is about one-third the size of Illinois. It is approximately 45 miles wide and 145 miles long.

IM4Him: When Pastor Scott brought out that fancy present, I thought he was going to talk about Christmas. He started talking about Jesus' birth. But then he talked about how the Jews' perspective of the Messiah was so different from what really happened. I actually thought that he and Mr. Gifford had shared their notes.

PHETI: Yeah, his talk fit right into the topic of our paper. Just like Pastor Scott said, although the Jewish people lacked a leader, they were unified by their religious doctrines and the promises made to them by Abraham. They believed that they had been chosen by God to fulfill a special mission in the world. They were just waiting for God to act.

QTee: I can certainly understand how they felt when they came under the rule of Rome. I'm sure that they couldn't understand why God was allowing all the oppression and hard times.

PHETI: So, like Mr. Gifford said, they were looking for a savior who would defeat the Romans. The Jews believed that Jerusalem, instead of Rome, should be the center of the world. Jesus was just not the type of messiah they expected.

IM4Him: You're right. The Jews were not sure how the Messiah would do it, but they were confident He would overthrow the Romans. There were even false messiahs that tried to lead rebellions against the Romans.

PHETI: Pastor Scott was exactly right. If we don't have the right perspective on events, we can draw the wrong conclusions. The prophecies in the Old Testament were very clear about the Messiah. The prophecies told about His birth, life, teaching, death and even His resurrection. But the Jews just didn't pay attention.

QTee: There were even miracles at the time of Jesus' birth—the virgin birth—and the birth of John the Baptist. But Jesus was not what the Jews had in mind.

PHETI: I'll bet the Jews were really confused when Jesus claimed to be both man and God. They didn't expect their Messiah to be the perfect God-Man. But, like Pastor Scott said, Jesus was called Immanuel, which means "God with us."

QTee: He really helped me understand the word *incarnation* when he read John 1:14—"And the Word became flesh and dwelt among us, and we beheld His glory, the glory as of the only begotten of the Father, full of grace and truth." I'm sure the Jewish people never imagined that the Messiah would "become flesh" like them.

 IM4Him: I wrote down something else that meant a lot to me. The Bible says that by His incarnation, Jesus accomplished these four great things on our behalf.

 PHETI: I liked the list of examples of Jesus' humanity in the Book of John. Did you guys get all of them?

QTee: I think so. Jesus grew up in Nazareth (1:45), traveled with His mother and brothers (2:12), asked for a drink of water in Samaria (4:7), crossed the Sea of Galilee in a boat (6:1), spat on the ground to make mud for a blind man's eyes (9:6), wept over Lazarus' death (11:35), washed the disciples' feet (13:5), died and was buried (19:30,42), and even after the resurrection He bore nail marks in His hands (20:20,27).

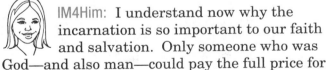 IM4Him: I understand now why the incarnation is so important to our faith and salvation. Only someone who was God—and also man—could pay the full price for our sin. Only someone who was tempted just like us—but remained sinless—could help us with our own spiritual struggles. It's like Pastor Scott said, Jesus was not simply a man who was a great teacher—He was the God of all eternity, the promised Messiah.

 PHETI: I just keep thinking about having the right perspective on things that happen in my own life. Although the Jews were expecting a messiah who would lead them to victory over the Romans, that's not what God had in mind for them. God provided a Messiah who would redeem them from their sins.

FILE SHARING

1. Though He was rich, yet for our sake He became poor so that He might make us rich (2 Corinthians 8:9 and Ephesians 1:18-21).

2. He became of no reputation so that we, without any merit or reputation of our own, might become known to God (Philippians 2:7 and Romans 4:6-7).

3. God made Christ, who knew no sin, to be sin so that we sinners might become the righteousness of God (2 Corinthians 5:21 and Romans 8:1-3).

4. God set the pattern for all believers in Christ to experience the incarnation through the indwelling Holy Spirit (1 John 3:24 and Colossians 1:27).

QTee: God always seems to understand what we need better than we do. I liked the way Pastor Scott explained it. When he first wrote the words "perspective," "God cares" and "incarnation" on the overhead, I didn't see the connection. But then it all made sense when he drew the arrow from the word "perspective" to the words "God cares" and "incarnation."

PHETI: It's just like a person to always look out for himself or to do what's best for himself. But God's perspective is to care for us. That's why He became flesh. Because He became like us, He can understand our troubles and struggles.

QTee: It is so great to know that God has always cared for us. That's why He sent His Son. I wrote down Romans 5:8 and 10: "But God demonstrates His own love toward us, in that while we were still sinners, Christ died for us. Much more then, having now been justified by His blood, we shall be saved from wrath through Him."

PHETI: I need a favor. Remember the story that Pastor Scott told us tonight? When I got home, I wrote it out so that I wouldn't forget it. Here's what I wrote. Tell me if I got all the facts straight.

QTee: That sounds right to me. It was a really good story, and I felt sorry for Mr. Morgan. Being rejected really does hurt.

IM4Him: But we know it's God's perspective that really counts. Even though we are sometimes rejected by other people, God always accepts us. All who have received Jesus Christ as personal Savior are totally accepted by the God of the universe.

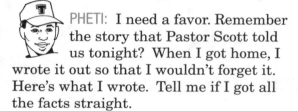

FILE SHARING

Many years ago, a young preacher named G. Campbell Morgan delivered a sermon to a panel of powerful church leaders who were to judge his fitness to be a minister. The men were not impressed with what they heard. As a result, they turned him down.

Knowing that his father was anxiously waiting at home to hear the good news, Mr. Morgan wired his father only one word: REJECTED.

Soon he received a reply from his father. It said: REJECTED ON EARTH, BUT ACCEPTED IN HEAVEN. DAD.

G. Campbell Morgan became a world-famous teacher and author. But he never forgot the pain of being rejected.

QUESTFILE 4.1

Life Principles Summarize one important life principle from each of the individuals you have studied this week.

ZACHARIAS

_____

_____

GABRIEL

_____

_____

ELIZABETH

_____

_____

NEIGHBORS AND RELATIVES

_____

_____

CAESAR AUGUSTUS

_____

_____

INNKEEPER

_____

_____

JOSEPH

_____

_____

ANGELS WHO APPEARED TO THE SHEPHERDS

_____

_____

SHEPHERDS

_____

_____

SIMEON

_____

_____

ANNA

_____

_____

MARY

_____

_____

The Miracle of the Incarnation

Summarize what you have learned about the incarnation of Christ.

Meaning of the word

_____

_____

_____

Meaning in relation to Jesus Christ

_____

_____

_____

Evidence that Jesus was human

1. _____

2. _____

3. _____

4. _____

5. _____

Evidence that Jesus was God

1. _____

2. _____

3. _____

4. _____

5. _____

Truths related to the incarnation of Christ

1. _____

2. _____

3. _____

4. _____

5. _____

How believers in Jesus Christ experience the incarnation

_____

_____

How these truths apply to my life

_____

_____

Christ in You   Interact with your parents or another adult mentor to develop a list of five things that would be true in your home life if the incarnation were evident on a daily basis.

1. _____

   _____

   _____

2. _____

   _____

   _____

3. _____

   _____

   _____

4. _____

   _____

   _____

5. _____

   _____

   _____

A MODEL CHILD

QuestTruth

Jesus Christ developed as a normal youth, having laid aside His divine nature. Thus, He serves as an example of growing mentally, physically, socially and spiritually.

QTee: It's been just awful! It all started with our lab experiment yesterday—the one with the messy worms. I told my parents about it at dinner. When I complained about how the experiment messed up my nails, my mom said, "I wish you would take care of your clothes as well as you take care of your nails." Then my dad joined in, "You paid way too much for those clothes last weekend. I can't afford new clothes every week just so you can wear the latest style."

They didn't want to listen to me. They just started in criticizing me. I really love my parents, but it seems like our talks always end up in an argument.

Gr8-1: So, all that happened last night? I noticed you weren't having a good day today. Did you get things settled with your parents?

QTee: Well, no. Everybody got the silent treatment this morning. They could tell that I was angry with them. When I got to school, Mrs. Edin met me coming in the door and she asked me what was wrong. It really surprised me.

Gr8-1: Didn't you expect her to notice? After all, as your counselor she's always on the lookout. Did she embarrass you?

QTee: No. But since I had study hall first hour, she asked me to come to her office. I didn't mind too much because she's really nice. But I wasn't in the mood to talk about what happened.

Gr8-1: Sometimes it helps me to talk. Just hearing myself explain a problem gives me a better perspective. What did Mrs. Edin say?

FACTOID

The city of Nazareth is so obscure that it is not mentioned once in the Old Testament.

QTee: Well, she said too many people expect life to be like the glorified catalogs they receive in the mail—life without conflict, misunderstanding, or criticism. They expect to have everything they want. They expect everything to be perfect. But, like she said, life is not like a catalog. It's messy and frustrating, just like the conflicts between parents and their children.

She then told me about a survey she read that asked teenagers to list the things they didn't like about their parents. I wrote down the top five responses.

1. Teens dislike parental anger.
2. Teens dislike pessimism and negativism in their parents.
3. Teens dislike constantly being nagged by their parents.
4. Teens dislike parents who act like teenagers.
5. Teens dislike it when parents show favoritism among their children.

 Gr8-1: Sounds like great information; you and Mrs. Edin had a good conversation. But why has the day been so awful? I still don't really understand.

 QTee: Our talk was good. I really appreciated everything she said. Even without discussing my specific problem, it made me feel better. But then I went to Bible second hour, and I couldn't believe today's lesson.

 Gr8-1: Yeah, we're studying the life of Jesus. But what's wrong with that? I don't get the connection.

QTee: Mr. Gifford started class by writing Ephesians 6:1-4 on the board— "Children, obey your parents in the Lord, for this is right. 'Honor your father and mother,' which is the first Commandment with promise: 'that it may be well with you and you may live long on the earth.' And you, fathers, do not provoke your children to wrath, but bring them up in the training and admonition of the Lord."

Then he told us that Paul wrote those words because he knew that there would be disagreements between parents and their children. It was almost like my parents had called Mr. Gifford and told him what had happened.

Gr8-1: You know they didn't do that. You're just upset. In our class Mr. Gifford said that the Bible doesn't give much information about Jesus' boyhood. He got my attention, though, when he talked about Jesus as a political refugee. I knew that Mary and Joseph took Jesus to Egypt to avoid King Herod's decree—the one that ordered boys under two years of age to be killed. I just never thought about Jesus as a political refugee.

QTee: Mr. Gifford told our class about that also. But it was the second event— the one that happened when Jesus was 12—that was really interesting.

Gr8-1: You know, I missed some notes about that second event. Since Mr. Gifford will quiz both classes on what he said, it'd help if you would go over your notes with me.

QTee: No problem. Mr. Gifford said that the longest story of what happened during Jesus' boyhood is recorded in Luke 2:40-52. Here are my notes.

FILE SHARING

1. *Jesus went with His parents to celebrate the Passover in Jerusalem. Although His parents had probably gone to Jerusalem each year to celebrate the Passover, Jesus was not able to go until He reached 12 years old.*

2. *Jesus grew up in a family that faithfully observed the Jewish feasts and customs. Passover was a one-day feast, followed immediately by the week-long Feast of Unleavened Bread. The Passover and Feast of Unleavened Bread were annual reminders of how God had spared Israel and brought them out of the land of Egypt.*

3. *According to Exodus 23:14-16, the Feast of Unleavened Bread was one of three feasts that the Jews were to celebrate each year. In addition to the Feast of Unleavened Bread, they celebrated the Feast of Harvest, an expression of gratitude to God for all the grain He had provided, and the Feast of Ingathering, a thanksgiving for the final harvest of the year.*

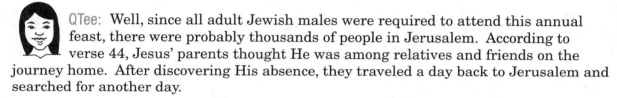

4. Bar mitzvah *means "son of the commandment."* A bar mitzvah *ceremony celebrates a Jewish boy's 13th birthday, when he reaches the age of religious duty and responsibility. Usually,* Mr. Gifford said, *boys celebrated their first Passover at age 12, in preparation for their* bar mitzvah. *That's why Jesus was in Jerusalem. By attending Passover, Jesus was taking His first step to being recognized as an adult in the Jewish community.*

Gr8-1: Obviously, Jesus remained in Jerusalem when his parents left at the end of the Passover. Joseph and Mary did not notice His absence until they had traveled a full day. How is that possible? My parents would have missed me immediately.

QTee: Well, since all adult Jewish males were required to attend this annual feast, there were probably thousands of people in Jerusalem. According to verse 44, Jesus' parents thought He was among relatives and friends on the journey home. After discovering His absence, they traveled a day back to Jerusalem and searched for another day.

Gr8-1: I remember that Mary and Joseph found Jesus in the Temple "sitting in the midst of the teachers, listening to them and asking them questions" (Luke 2:46). Of course, Jesus wanted to know why they were so concerned. That's why he said to Mary and Joseph, "Did you not know that I must be about My Father's business?" (Luke 2:49). That's when Mr. Gifford asked us to describe what kind of student Jesus was.

QTee: He asked our class that question too. I had never really thought much about it. I just supposed that Jesus already knew everything when He was born or that He could learn anything without studying.

Gr8-1: Remember what Mr. Gifford said. Although Jesus asked questions that astonished the teachers, He still went through the process of education. The rabbis were scholars of Judaism; some were even members of the Council, the governing body of Judea. Not only the rabbis were astonished with Jesus' understanding and answers, but so were His parents.

QTee: Then they returned to Nazareth after leaving the Temple, and Jesus continued the normal process of growing up. According to Mr. Gifford, that's why this brief account of Jesus' boyhood concludes with "And Jesus increased in wisdom and stature, and in favor with God and men" (Luke 2:52). Until class today, I hadn't realized that there is so little information on Jesus' boyhood in the Bible.

Gr8-1: I thought it was really interesting when Mr. Gifford pointed out that Luke 2:52 made it clear that Jesus obeyed the Fifth Commandment—"Honor your father and your mother, that your days may be long upon the land which the Lord your God is giving you" (Exodus 20:12). Like he said, Jesus did not stop being God in order to become man. At the same time, He was completely human and had a normal childhood.

 QTee: That was a great point. But then Mr. Gifford started talking about the relationship between children and their parents. That's when I was sure that my parents had talked with him this morning. He said that all families have disagreements. But God's Word explains how parents and children are to respond to each other. Just like Exodus 20:12 tells children to honor their parents, Ephesians 6:4 tells parents "do not provoke your children to wrath, but bring them up in the training and admonition of the Lord."

Gr8-1: I really liked what he said about how honoring your parents is a gift that you can give them each day. The guidelines he gave were great, but I didn't get them all down.

QTee: No problem. I realized I really needed them, so here they are.

FILE SHARING

1. Respect the role your parents play in your life. Real life should not be like the television shows where children treat their parents with disrespect.

2. Obey without having to be asked a second time. If your parents are repeatedly asking you to do something, don't consider that as nagging.

3. Try to talk to your parents, instead of "grunting" your responses. Single-syllable words are not considered "talking" to your parents.

4. Always tell the truth. Although you might not deliberately lie to your parents, you might try to deceive them—like when you don't tell the whole truth or you leave out essential facts to make things look better than they really are.

5. *Don't put down your parents in front of your friends. When you put down your parents, you show disloyalty to the longest-lasting relationship you will ever have in this world.*

6. *Forgive your parents when they fail. It's wrong to hold grudges or give them the silent treatment after they have made a mistake.*

7. *Don't take advantage of your parents. Love and honor your parents for who they are, not just for what they have done and can do for you.*

8. *Return the care and understanding they have given to you. When your parents face difficulties, they need your understanding, not your criticism.*

9. *Respect the advice your parents give you. Even though you may not agree, your parents are concerned about what's best for you.*

10. *Make it a practice to express your appreciation to your parents. Nothing honors parents more than knowing that their children are grateful for the family God has given them.*

Gr8-1: Thanks for your help. I'm sorry your day was tough. It's never fun when things aren't going well with your parents.

QTee: Don't worry, I'm doing much better now. Actually, I'm glad that all of this happened today. The Lord is teaching me a lot. SYL

Home Improvement
Later this week as part of Bible class, you are expected to discuss with your parents ways to improve family relationships. In preparation, list three to five items under each heading. Your parents have been asked to complete a similar exercise. Discuss with your parents what expectations are similar on both of your lists, then discuss the unique items that appear on each list. Use the opportunity to gain a mutual understanding and to develop a plan of action that can lead to increased harmony in your home.

What I think my parent(s) would most like to see improved in me:

_____
_____
_____
_____
_____
_____
_____

What I would most like to see improved in my parent(s):

_____
_____
_____
_____
_____
_____

A plan of action my parents and I can agree to:

_____

_____

_____

_____

_____

_____

_____

_____

_____

_____

_____

_____   _____
Student's signature   *Parent's signature*

QUESTFILE 5.2

10 Ways to Honor Your Parents   In your student text, Mr. Gifford indicated the following 10 ways that you could fulfill the Fifth Commandment to honor your mother and father. As you read each of these 10 statements, circle the number that best represents how well you are doing in this area in your life today. Then write a prayer asking God to help you improve in the areas you are weak.

1. RESPECT THE ROLE PARENTS PLAY IN MY LIFE.

Always					Sometimes					Never
10	9	8	7	6	5	4	3	2	1	0

2. OBEY WITHOUT HAVING TO BE ASKED TO DO SOMETHING A SECOND TIME.

Always					Sometimes					Never
10	9	8	7	6	5	4	3	2	1	0

3. TALK TO MY PARENTS, INSTEAD OF "GRUNTING" MY RESPONSES.

Always					Sometimes					Never
10	9	8	7	6	5	4	3	2	1	0

4. ALWAYS TELL THE TRUTH.

Always					Sometimes					Never
10	9	8	7	6	5	4	3	2	1	0

5. DON'T PUT DOWN MY PARENTS IN FRONT OF MY FRIENDS.

Always					Sometimes					Never
10	9	8	7	6	5	4	3	2	1	0

6. FORGIVE MY PARENTS WHEN THEY FAIL.

Always   Sometimes   Never
10   9   8   7   6   5   4   3   2   1   0

7. DON'T TAKE ADVANTAGE OF MY PARENTS.

Always   Sometimes   Never
10   9   8   7   6   5   4   3   2   1   0

8. RETURN THE CARE AND UNDERSTANDING THEY HAVE GIVEN ME.

Always   Sometimes   Never
10   9   8   7   6   5   4   3   2   1   0

9. RESPECT THE ADVICE MY PARENTS GIVE ME.

Always   Sometimes   Never
10   9   8   7   6   5   4   3   2   1   0

10. MAKE IT A PRACTICE TO EXPRESS MY APPRECIATION TO MY PARENTS.

Always   Sometimes   Never
10   9   8   7   6   5   4   3   2   1   0

Dear Lord, please help me to . . . _____

_____

_____

_____

QUESTFILE 5.3

Finding Balance   In each block list at least three more things you should do, or discontinue doing, in order to obtain a better balance in your life.

MENTAL

1. *Grow in wisdom*

2.

3.

4.

PHYSICAL

1. *Grow strong physically*

2.

3.

4.

SOCIAL

1. *Grow in relationships with other people*

2.

3.

4.

SPIRITUAL

1. *Grow in my relationship with God*

2.

3.

4.

A VOICE IN THE DESERT

QUESTTRUTH

Those who follow God will experience persecution from those who do not know Him. Their responsibility is to live righteously, maintain joy and remain faithful.

2B4Givn: Can I help? I hear you're in trouble. I talked with Mom today, and she told me what happened at school.

IM4Him: But I didn't do it! My lab partner put the frog's "spare parts" in Beth's backpack. I couldn't help laughing. I told Mom and Dad the truth, but I still got into trouble.

2B4Givn: Listen, while telling the truth is always the right thing to do, it doesn't mean that it will always keep you out of trouble. Have you ever read *Fox's Book of Martyrs*?

IM4Him: I've never read it. When I saw the book, it seemed old and difficult to read. What's it about?

2B4Givn: The book was written by John Foxe, and the first English edition was published in 1563. It tells the stories of hundreds of people who were tortured and killed because of their faith in Jesus Christ. They did nothing to deserve punishment. But they found themselves in trouble for just telling the truth.

IM4Him: Sounds like me, all right. I didn't mean to cause a problem. Are you suggesting that I'm acting like a martyr?

2B4Givn: No, of course not. But, like I said, just because you tell the truth, you are not immune to trouble. In my New Testament Survey course, I'm doing a paper on John the Baptist. He's a perfect example. He was put in prison by Herod and eventually beheaded for only one reason: He told the truth!

IM4Him: We're studying John the Baptist in our Bible class too. I really like his rugged appearance and fearless preaching. What is your paper about?

2B4Givn: The focus of my paper is the special assignment God gave him. You see, John the Baptist played an important role in announcing the coming Messiah. Jesus said about him, "Assuredly, I say to you, among those born of women there has not risen one greater than John the Baptist" (Matthew 11:11). Can I show you what I've already written?

The story of John's life began just six months before the angel appeared to the virgin Mary (Luke 1:26). His father, Zacharias, was one of the many volunteer priests who served in the Temple two weeks a year, and then lived the rest of the time at his own home in the countryside. Zacharias was not really an important man. He was given the honor of serving in the Temple because he was a descendent of Aaron. This privilege was usually passed from father to son. Certainly, it was Zacharias' hope that his son would follow in his footsteps. Maybe, Zacharias thought, his son might even become a priest some day.

But his dream was not to be—at least in human terms. He and Elizabeth had remained childless into their old age, until the angel Gabriel announced the birth of the child who was to prepare the way of the Lord. Although Zacharias knew that God had His hand upon John, he had no idea the important role his son would play in God's plan of redemption.

Even though the Bible tells us nothing about John's childhood, we can conclude that his interests were different from other boys his age. Perhaps his parents died while he was young, forcing him to become self-reliant. When he reached adulthood, he chose to live in the wilderness. He ate wild honey and locusts. He was clothed in camel's hair with a leather belt around his waist. When the time was right, he began the task God had sent him to accomplish. He began to preach in the areas near the Jordan River.

The content of John's message was not really new. According to Luke 3:10-14, John encouraged people to turn to righteousness in preparation for the coming Kingdom of God. He told them to give food to those who had no food. He told the tax collector to "Collect no more than what is appointed for you." He told the soldiers not to use their power to falsely accuse others or receive more wages than they should.

The Jewish people were so impressed with John's teaching that they wondered if he was the expected Messiah. However, John quickly ended their speculation when he said, "I indeed baptize you with water; but One mightier than I is coming, whose sandal strap I am not worthy to loose. He will baptize you with the Holy Spirit and fire."

Although the content of John's message was not new, there were several things about his preaching that were new. John preached with a sense of urgency. "Repent," he said, "for the Kingdom of heaven is at hand!" (Matthew 3:2). John wanted his hearers to know that they had to take action now. They could not continue to put off their need to repent of their sins.

IM4Him: It sounds like John the Baptist was an evangelist. The focus of his ministry was the personal responsibility of an individual for his own actions.

2B4Givn: Although the Old Testament taught individual responsibility for behavior, the majority of the Jews believed that their relationship with God was secure because they were descendants of Abraham. Here are some additional notes.

FILE SHARING

John warned the people not to place their hope in Abraham—"And do not think to say to yourselves, 'We have Abraham as our father.' For I say to you that God is able to raise up children to Abraham from these stones" (Matthew 3:9). He urged them to repent of their sins and make a personal commitment to God.

There was a final, unique aspect to John's preaching. He realized that God had sent him to be a forerunner, to prepare the way for the Messiah. Seven times the New Testament records John's announcement that the one to follow him would be grater than him (Matthew 3:11; Mark 1:7; Luke 3:16; John 1:27,29-31,32-34; Acts 13:25).

John the Baptist attracted a huge following. This was not only because he was a great teacher, but also because he was unlike any prophet they had ever seen. The multitudes were fascinated by the way he dressed, the passion of his preaching, and his challenge to everyone to repent. Some came because of their spiritual needs. Many came just to see for themselves what he was like. They continued to gossip about whether he might be the Messiah, and they waited to see what would happen next!

Matthew 3:13 states, "Then Jesus came from Galilee to John at the Jordan to be baptized by him." John immediately objected, saying, "I need to be baptized by You, and are You coming to me?" (Matthew 3:14). But Jesus reminded him that He had to fulfill all righteousness [accomplish God's mission] and that it was important for John to baptize Him. John's objection to baptizing Jesus may have been based on one simple fact: John knew that Jesus had no need to repent! He knew that Jesus had obeyed the laws and followed the ways of God. But Jesus insisted, so John baptized Jesus.

Immediately upon being baptized, the Spirit of God, represented by a dove, descended upon Jesus. At the same time, "a voice came from heaven, saying, 'This is My beloved Son, in whom I am well pleased'" (Matthew 3:17). There was no question now. John knew that Jesus was the Messiah. John had fulfilled the assignment that God had given to him. He had prepared the way for the Messiah, Jesus Christ.

The baptism of Jesus launched His public ministry. This is the last time we hear about John the Baptist until we learn that he had been imprisoned and later killed (Matthew 14; Mark 6; Luke 9). According to the gospel accounts, Herod Antipas imprisoned John because he had condemned the king's illicit relationship with his brother's wife. The woman, Herodias, hated John and wanted to kill him. But Herod "feared John, knowing that he was a just and holy man, and he protected him" (Mark 6:20).

IM4Him: You said that John the Baptist got into trouble because he told the truth. Is this what you were talking about?

2B4Givn: John the Baptist was put into prison because of his preaching. He told the truth about man's need to repent and that Jesus was the Messiah. Of course, Herodias wanted him killed. Herod, though, did not want to incite the people. Let's go back to my notes.

Unfortunately, Herod's lust soon got him into trouble again. It was common for Herod to have celebrations that included drinking, gluttony, and sexual orgies. At his birthday party, Herodias' daughter danced for the king. Herod enjoyed the dance so much that he said to her, "Ask me whatever you want, and I will give it to you" (Mark 6:22). He then swore to her, "Whatever you ask me, I will give you, up to half my kingdom" (Mark 6:23). Obviously, he was not only overtaken by her sensuous dancing, but also by all he had been drinking.

The daughter went to her mother to find out what she should request from the king. Herodias did not have to think for long. This was her opportunity for revenge against John the Baptist. Immediately after meeting with Herodias, her daughter returned to the king and said, "I want you to give me at once the head of John the Baptist on a platter" (Mark 6:25).

Herod was shocked! He knew that John was a prophet and a holy man. He looked around at his guests who had heard him make the promise. He was trapped. Although he knew he should not honor her request, Herod was unwilling to be embarrassed. He ordered that John be beheaded and that his head be brought to the banquet room on a platter.

John's life did not come to this tragic end because he had done something wrong. He had lived a righteous life. He had been obedient to God. He preached that people needed to repent of their sins. He proclaimed the coming of Jesus as the Messiah. Yet his attempt to live a holy life got him into trouble, ultimately leading to his death.

IM4Him: Even though I didn't do anything wrong, and I told the truth, I can see how Mom and Dad thought that I might have been involved.

 2B4Givn: Sometimes, even if we don't do something wrong ourselves, we make choices that can get us into trouble.

 IM4Him: Yeah, by laughing at what happened it looked like I was guilty of putting the frog's "spare parts" in Beth's backpack too. Even though it was kind of funny, I shouldn't have laughed.

 2B4Givn: As I was doing my research on John the Baptist, I found an interesting story about the choices we make. It's really a good illustration. Let me share it with you.

FILE SHARING

New Direction Needed

There was once a boy who was on his way to a friend's house. He could take several streets that would lead to his destination. So he chose one and began walking down it. All of sudden, he fell into a hole filled with muddy water. He never even saw the hole. Though he was able to pull himself out, his clothes were covered with mud and other debris. He had to go home to change clothes.

Soon he was back to the streets that led to his friend's house. Since he knew where the hole was, he decided to go down the same street. As he approached the hole, his curiosity caused him to want a closer look. As he stepped closer to the hole, the earth beneath his feet gave way, and he again plunged into the hole. As before, he was covered with mud from head to foot. So he went home to change his clothes.

An hour later, he returned to the same area and was faced with his original choice: which street to take to his friend's house. He once again chose the same street, but he was determined not to go anywhere near the hole. In fact, he turned to his right to go around it. However, his eyes were so fixed upon the hole that he didn't see an even bigger hole directly in his path. In a matter of seconds, he was up to his neck in filthy water. He struggled out of the hole, angry with himself for not seeing this new—and even larger—hole! He made his way home again, hoping he still had some clean clothes to wear.

Finally, he returned to the same set of streets for a fourth time. Once again he looked down the street that he had traveled three times before. But this time he made a different decision. He chose to walk down another street. His example teaches an obvious lesson. Only a fool would continue traveling the path that leads to trouble; a new direction is needed.

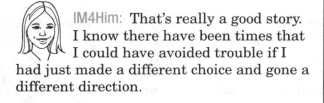 IM4Him: That's really a good story. I know there have been times that I could have avoided trouble if I had just made a different choice and gone a different direction.

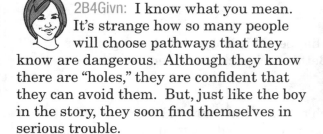 2B4Givn: I know what you mean. It's strange how so many people will choose pathways that they know are dangerous. Although they know there are "holes," they are confident that they can avoid them. But, just like the boy in the story, they soon find themselves in serious trouble.

 IM4Him: But, in the case of John the Baptist, it is true that we can choose the right path and yet get into trouble. Still, it's better to choose the right way. Eventually, with God, things will turn out okay.

2B4Givn: Jesus gave us the image of the paths in Matthew 7:13-14. One is broad and leads to destruction. Jesus reminds us that this is the path that most people choose. He then says that there is another path, one that is narrow and difficult. However, this is the path that leads to life. Unfortunately, He says, there are few who choose this path.

 IM4Him: I know there's a lot of trouble in the world today because people have chosen the broad way of the ungodly. Because of the choices they make, they are walking down the path to destruction.

2B4Givn: But Jesus wants us to walk down a different path. He encourages us to make the more difficult decision—to choose the way of righteousness. Of course, that doesn't mean that we'll never have troubles. John the Baptist is a good example. But it does mean that we will be walking down the path that will lead to eternal life and fellowship with God. It is the only path that will keep us out of REAL TROUBLE.

QUESTFILE 6.1

The Kingdom of God Is Near John called people to repentance, saying that the Kingdom of God was near. You have already studied the kind of kingdom most Jews were hoping to have. But God had a very different kingdom in mind. Read Daniel 7:13-14; Isaiah 61:1-3; and Zechariah 14:9 and explain what the real kingdom was to be like in the four areas mentioned. Then contrast these to what the Jews wanted.

God's Kingdom

The desire of the Jews

spiritual

for all

in heaven

forever

In the future, Jesus will return as the triumphant King of heaven and earth, and thus fulfill all prophecies related to the Kingdom of God. At this time, His spiritual kingdom is in the hearts of believers.

John's Message Study Matthew 3:1-12; Luke 3:4-18; John 1:6-8; and 3:27-30. Sort the phrases from the transparency to the categories listed. Be prepared to justify your answers.

A. *Information about Jesus, the coming Messiah*

1. _____

_____

2. _____

_____

3. _____

_____

4. _____

_____

5. _____

_____

6. _____

_____

7. _____

_____

B. *Information about himself (John)*

1. _____

_____

2. _____

_____

3. _____

_____

4. _____

_____

5. _____

_____

6. _____

_____

7. _____

_____

8. _____

_____

C. Information to and about his hearers

Jewish people in general

1. _____

_____

2. _____

_____

3. _____

_____

4. _____

_____

Pharisees and Sadducees

1. _____

_____

2. _____

_____

3. _____

_____

4. _____

_____

Tax collectors

1. _____

_____

Soldiers

1. _____

_____

2. _____

_____

Herod Antipas

1. _____

_____

2. _____

_____

Trails to Trouble

Troubles basically happen for the four reasons listed below. Discuss and record experiences in your family related to these areas. Then on the next page discuss and record better ways to handle the situations.

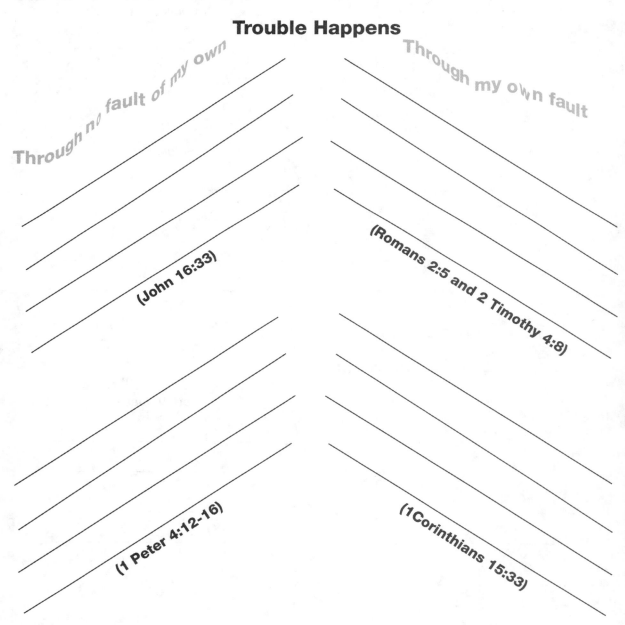

Trouble Happens

Through no fault of my own

Through my own fault

(John 16:33)

(Romans 2:5 and 2 Timothy 4:8)

(1 Peter 4:12-16)

(1Corinthians 15:33)

Ways to best avoid trouble: _____

_____

_____

_____

_____

_____

What to do while in trouble: _____

_____

_____

_____

_____

_____

Ways to get out of trouble: _____

_____

_____

_____

_____

_____

CALLING DISCIPLES

QuestTruth

Jesus called twelve disciples to assist in ministry and to bear witness of the gospel to the world. Believers today are called to fulfill similar purposes.

 PHETI: Hey, where were you this afternoon? I went to your locker after school and you weren't there.

 Gr8-1: Sorry I missed you. I stopped by to see my uncle this afternoon on my way home from school. You remember my mom's brother, right?

 PHETI: You mean Pastor Alvarez over on 31st Street? I almost forgot that he's your uncle. Why did you need to see him?

 Gr8-1: He said I could see him any time I needed someone to talk to. Today wasn't really a good day for me. Basketball tryouts are over, and I've been looking forward to being a part of the team ever since I was in middle school.

 PHETI: Yeah, I remember. We used to play every day at the park. Anyway, I thought you made the team.

Gr8-1: I did, but barely. Back in 7th grade I was the tallest guy on the team. Coach Jay made me the center that year. The next year I wasn't the tallest, but I was still pretty big. I played the forward position. This year's "cut list" was posted this afternoon, and I barely made the team. Actually, I was the last person on the list.

PHETI: I've seen you play. You're pretty good—you're quick and handle the ball well. Your outside shots are great.

 Gr8-1: My shooting is pretty good, but I haven't grown any taller. I'm actually the same height as when I was in 7th grade. Can you believe that? I was hoping to be a part of the summer missions basketball team next year. Now, I doubt if I'll even make the team.

PHETI: Come to think of it, you are still the same height as when we first met. I never really gave it much thought. It sounds like something else is bothering you. Spill it, bro.

 Gr8-1: I got a C- on the physical science exam—not exactly stellar for a would-be medical missionary. I'll probably never get into medical school.

 PHETI: Don't give up too soon; you still have plenty of time. Is that why you went to see your uncle?

 Gr8-1: I just needed to talk to someone. Besides, he was a really good basketball player in college. I knew he would understand. He reminded me that there are challenges at every stage of life. As we successfully meet these challenges, we move on to the next stage of life.

 PHETI: It's good to have somebody to talk to. What kind of challenges was he talking about?

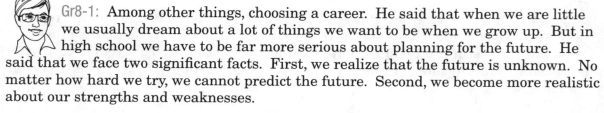 Gr8-1: Among other things, choosing a career. He said that when we are little we usually dream about a lot of things we want to be when we grow up. But in high school we have to be far more serious about planning for the future. He said that we face two significant facts. First, we realize that the future is unknown. No matter how hard we try, we cannot predict the future. Second, we become more realistic about our strengths and weaknesses.

 PHETI: You mean, like you're not going to grow any taller? Sounds like he's pretty straight with the truth—no sugar coating.

 Gr8-1: That's why I like him. Anyway, he started talking about Jesus' disciples. As young Jewish boys, they had learned about the expected Messiah and probably wondered about things like what He would be like or why He had not yet come to deliver His people.

PHETI: I never thought about Jesus' disciples being teenagers. It's hard to imagine. I guess none of them had any idea that they would be a part of the Messiah's inner circle.

Gr8-1: He spent a lot of time talking about Jesus' disciples. I took notes in my journal. I'll share them.

FILE SHARING

• Mark was the first one to record that Jesus selected twelve followers (Mark 1:16-20). They assisted Jesus throughout His ministry, like when the Lord performed the miracle of the feeding of the 4,000 (Matthew 15:38). Probably their most important function was to serve as witnesses to the miracles that proved Jesus was the Son of God.

• After the resurrection of Jesus, eleven of the disciples gathered to select a replacement for Judas Iscariot. According to Peter, certain characteristics had to be true of a disciple. "Therefore, of these men who have accompanied us all the time that the Lord Jesus went in and out among us, beginning from the baptism of John to that day when He was taken up from us, one of these must become a witness with us of His resurrection" (Acts 1:21-22). In other words, any new disciple chosen must have traveled with Jesus since His baptism, been an eyewitness to His miracles, and seen His resurrection.

PHETI: I can see why that's so important. The disciples would become responsible for spreading the gospel throughout the known world. There was no room in early Christianity for myths and rumors. The story of Jesus could not be hearsay accounts based on local gossip. The testimonies had to be from those who were actually there, and they had to be accurate.

Gr8-1: My uncle asked me what criteria I would use if I'd had the responsibility to choose Jesus' disciples. That was a hard question.

PHETI: Well, most leaders would want to make sure that they were well educated, came from good families, and were very religious.

Gr8-1: That's exactly what he said. But the twelve disciples lacked most, if not all, of those criteria. My uncle gave me a little pamphlet he wrote that tells about each of the disciples. Give me a sec.

The Twelve Disciples

ANDREW, the brother of Peter, lived in Capernaum and was a fisherman before Jesus called him. Originally he was a disciple of John the Baptist (Mark 1:16-18). It was Andrew who brought his brother Peter to Jesus (John 1:40). Andrew is most noted for his missionary focus. Matter of fact, he is claimed by three countries as their Patron Saint: Russia, Scotland and Greece. He was crucified on an X-shaped cross that has become known as Saint Andrew's Cross.

BARTHOLOMEW lived in Cana of Galilee. His name appears on every list of the disciples (Matthew 10:3; Mark 3:18; Luke 6:14; Acts 1:13). This was not a first name, however; it was his second name. His first name probably was Nathanael, whom Jesus called "an Israelite indeed, in whom is no deceit" (John 1:47). The New Testament gives us very little information about him. However, tradition says that he preached in India, and his death seems to have taken place there—being flayed alive with knives as a martyr for his Lord.

JAMES, THE ELDER, was the brother of John, the Apostle. His name never appears apart from that of his brother John. He was a fisherman when Jesus called him. His preaching ministry was focused in Jerusalem and Judea until he was beheaded by Herod Antipas in 44 A.D. (Acts 12:2). James, the Elder, was the first of the Twelve to become a martyr.

JAMES, THE LESSER, was the brother of the Apostle Jude. His title may refer to his age or to a small stature. According to tradition, he preached in Egypt and was crucified there. James was a man of strong character who preached the gospel with great passion. His style of preaching has often been compared to that of John the Baptist. Tradition indicates that after his crucifixion, his body was sawed into pieces.

JOHN, the Apostle, was also known as the Beloved Disciple. Like his brother James, he was a fisherman when the Lord called him. He wrote the Gospel of John, 1 John, 2 John, 3 John, and Revelation. He preached throughout Asia Minor before being banished to the Isle of Patmos, where he wrote the Book of Revelation. According to tradition, he was later freed and died a natural death near Ephesus at near 100 years of age.

John's second name was Boanerges, which means Son of Thunder. He and his brother James came from a more well-to-do family than the rest of the disciples. According to Mark 1:20, his father had hired servants in his fishing business. John and Peter often worked closely together in their preaching ministry.

FILE SHARING

JUDAS ISCARIOT betrayed Jesus for 30 pieces of silver and afterward hanged himself (Matthew 26:14,16). Judas is probably one of the most mysterious individuals in the New Testament. For centuries, Christians have wondered how anyone who was so close to Jesus, saw so many miracles and heard so much of the Lord's teachings, could ever betray Him into the hands of His enemies.

Judas was likely a Jewish Nationalist who followed in hopes that through Jesus they could overthrow the Romans. Obviously Judas was a covetous man who used his position with the Lord to increase his personal income. We will never know exactly why Judas betrayed his master. But it is important to remember that it was not his betrayal that ultimately put Jesus on the cross—it was our sins.

JUDE was the brother of James the Lesser. He is often known as the "man with three names." In Mark 3:18 he is called Thaddeus. In Matthew 10:3 he is called Lebbeus. In Luke 6:16 and Acts 1:13 he is called Judas the brother of James. He was also known as Judas the Zealot. In addition to writing the Book of Jude, he preached the gospel in Persia. Tradition teaches that he was killed with arrows while at Ararat, now the land of Turkey.

MATTHEW, or Levi, wrote the gospel that bears his name and died a martyr in Ethiopia. Although we know little about Matthew personally, we are told that he was a tax collector. The Jews hated tax collectors with a passion. To the devout Jew, God was the only one to whom it was right to pay tribute in taxes. To pay anyone else, especially corrupt Romans, was to infringe on the rights of God. The tax collectors were hated not just on religious grounds, but also because they were notoriously unjust.

In New Testament times, tax collectors were classified with harlots, Gentiles, and sinners (Matthew 18:17; 21:31,33; Mark 2:15-16; Luke 5:30). Yet Jesus saw the potential of this tax collector. He chose a man others hated and made him one of His disciples.

PETER was a fisherman along with his brother Andrew. He authored the two New Testament epistles that bear his name. Additionally, it's likely that he's responsible for the information in Mark's gospel. In every apostolic list, the name Peter is mentioned first. However, Peter had other names. His Greek name was Simon (Mark 1:16; John 1:40-41) and his Hebrew name was Cephas (1 Corinthians 1:12; 3:22; 9:5; and Galatians 2:9). The Greek meaning of Simon is "rock." The Hebrew meaning of Cephas is also "rock." Bar Jonah means son of Jonah, owner of a boat on the Sea of Galilee.

Among the Twelve, Peter was the fiery leader. He often served as the spokesman for the group. For example, it was he who asked how often he must forgive, inquired about the reward for those who followed Jesus, and first confessed Jesus as the Son of the Living God. Yet it was also Peter who denied Christ three times. After repentance, he became a chief leader in the early church. Peter was martyred on a cross, requesting to be crucified head downward. He believed that he was not worthy to die as his Lord had died.

PHILIP, a fisherman, came from Bethsaida, the same town from which Peter and Andrew came (John 1:44). As soon as he was called by Jesus, Philip went to tell Nathanael that "we have found Him of whom Moses in the Law, and also the prophets, wrote—Jesus of Nazareth, the son of Joseph." Philip was known for his simple, obedient faith in Christ. Tradition records that he died by hanging. While dying, he requested that his body be wrapped in papyrus and not in linen, for he was not worthy that even his dead body should be treated as the body of Jesus had been treated.

SIMON the Zealot is one of the least known of the followers of Jesus. The Zealots were fanatical Jewish Nationalists who fought to protect the purity of their faith. They hated the Romans and all that the Roman government represented. As a Zealot, Simon was devoted to the Jewish law and ceremonies. However, as a follower of Christ, he showed his ability to work with the other disciples to spread the gospel of repentance and love. Tradition says he was crucified.

THOMAS lived in Galilee, preached in Persia and India, and was martyred in India. He second name, Didymus, means twin and is similar to our word "ditto." He is most remembered as "Doubting Thomas" because he was unwilling to believe that Jesus had truly been raised from the dead until he saw the nail prints in His hands (John 20:25). Thomas then exclaimed, "My Lord and my God!" (John 20:28). His doubts were transformed into faith and he spent the rest of his life preaching the gospel.

 PHETI: Wow, that's a great tract! But the resumes for Jesus' disciples were not very impressive. Apparently Jesus wasn't looking for highly intelligent, wealthy, or well-connected fellows. He was looking for men who would obey and faithfully follow Him.

Gr8-1: Right! Then my uncle said there is a parallel between Jesus with His disciples and a basketball coach with his players. Both must get their players in shape so that they can work together as a team. During practice times, the basketball coach studies the abilities and strengths of each player. Based on what he sees, he makes decisions regarding who plays a certain position and who will get to start the game. Physical ability and mental attitude are usually the basis upon which the coach's decision is made.

 PHETI: Sounds like one of Coach Jay's lectures. Remember how he used each letter of the word "shape" to encourage us to prepare to serve the Lord.

 Gr8-1: I'm afraid you've lost me now. What does serving the Lord have to do with the letters in the word "shape"?

FACTOID

Judas Iscariot was the only one of the twelve disciples who was not from Galilee.

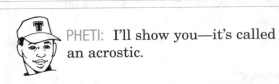

PHETI: I'll show you—it's called an acrostic.

FILE SHARING

Spiritual gift—God has given to each believer at least one spiritual gift (1 Corinthians 12:4-11). A spiritual gift is a special, God-given ability that He entrusts to each of His people in order to involve them in serving His Church. Ephesians 4:22 states that our gifts are "to prepare God's people for works of service so that the body of Christ may be built up." Given by the Holy Spirit, spiritual gifts remind us that we are one team (1Corinthians 12:11). Other spiritual gifts are listed in Romans 12.

Getting in shape to be a follower of Jesus means that we Christians must identify, develop and use the spiritual gift that God has given to us. This was the challenge Paul gave to young Timothy: "Therefore I remind you to stir up the gift of God which is in you through the laying on of my hands. For God has not given us a spirit of fear, but of power and of love and of a sound mind" (2 Timothy 1:6-7). As believers, God has already given us special abilities to do His work.

Heart for God—When Jesus refers to the "heart," He is talking about much more than the physical pump pushing blood throughout our body. Frequently, the word "heart" refers to our inner passions and priorities. Some people, Jesus reminds us, have a heart for the things of this world. Others have a heart for the things of God. That's why Jesus said in Matthew 6:21, "For where your treasure is, there your heart will be also."

Those who want to be in proper shape to serve Jesus must have a heart for the things of God. We must daily confess our sins and spend time developing a personal relationship with Him. One of the reasons that the disciples were effective is that they spent so much time with Jesus. The disciples soon developed the same passions and priorities as Jesus. They developed a heart for the things of God.

Abilities—In addition to a God-given spiritual gift, every person has natural skills—things that are easy for us to learn and do. Some may be very good organizers, while others may possess unusual strength or stamina. Some may have the ability to build or fix things, and still others the ability to paint or to write music. The important fact is that no two people are alike.

We need to carefully think about the abilities that God has given us. In order to be prepared to serve the Lord, we must be aware of the unique way that He has made us. Unless we use our abilities for Him, we will never be in shape to follow in the footsteps of Jesus.

Personality—Not only has God given us special gifts and abilities, He has given us each a unique personality—one that is only you. Think about the personalities of your friends.

- What one emotion best characterizes each person?
- Which is the most serious? Least serious? Most outgoing?
- Which one do you have the most fun with? Why?

Each of us has a different personality. We each respond to the daily events of life in very different ways. The different personalities of the disciples enabled them to complete the special assignments Jesus gave them.

Experiences—As we study the Bible we learn important lessons from the experiences of others. From the life of Abraham we learn the importance of faith. The story of Jonah reminds us that we cannot run from God. As we read about Mary we learn the meaning of humility. But God expects us also to learn from the experiences He has allowed us to have. They prepare us to be effective in the future.

That's it: **S. H. A. P. E.**

Gr8-1: Wow! That's quite a lesson. I finally understand something really important—just as Jesus took twelve ordinary people and made them His disciples, He can also use someone like me. I have to remember that God is always in control. And I have to be willing to get into shape to be His follower. Thanks for the good reminder!

FACTOID

Capernaum—Archaeological excavations have uncovered ruins of a synagogue built during Jesus' time. One block away is the foundation of an early church that excavators are convinced was built on the site of Peter's house, the place where Jesus healed Peter's mother-in-law and where He often stayed while in Capernaum.

QUESTFILE 7.1

Jesus' Temptation Read Matthew 4:1-11; Mark 1:12-13; and Luke 4:1-13. Answer the questions based on these passages and other Scripture with which you are familiar.

1. By whom was Jesus led into the wilderness? What was His purpose? _____

_____

_____

2. By whom was Jesus tempted? What was his purpose? _____

_____

_____

3. What was Jesus' physical state at the time of temptation? _____

_____

_____

4. Read 1 John 2:16 and classify Jesus' temptations based on:

1) the desires of the flesh: _____

2) the desires of the eyes: _____

3) the pride of life: _____

. . . "Man does not live on bread alone, but on every word that comes from the mouth of God."
–Matthew 4:4

5. Read Hebrews 4:14-16. In what ways was Jesus tempted like us? _____

_____

_____

6. What was Jesus' response to each temptation?

1) _____

2) _____

3) _____

7. Is temptation a sin? _____

8. Based on Jesus' experience, what are some important principles in handling temptation?

_____

_____

_____

_____

_____

_____

_____

. . . "Worship the Lord your God and serve Him only."
–Luke 4:8

Who Were the Disciples? Match the disciples with their descriptive phrases.

_____ 1. James, the Elder
_____ 2. Jude
_____ 3. Philip
_____ 4. Thomas
_____ 5. James, the Lesser
_____ 6. Peter
_____ 7. Judas Iscariot
_____ 8. Andrew
_____ 9. Matthew
_____ 10. John
_____ 11. Simon
_____ 12. Bartholomew

A. the Beloved Disciple
B. the man with several names
C. brought his brother Peter to Jesus
D. a tax collector
E. the first disciple to become a martyr
F. a member of a Jewish Nationalist group known as the Zealots
G. His first name was probably Nathanael.
H. His Greek and Hebrew names mean "rock."
I. known for his simple, obedient faith in Christ
J. brother of Jude
K. the "doubter"
L. betrayed Jesus for 30 pieces of silver

Family Chatroom/Different Strokes—Different Folks Discuss
with your parents or other adults their responses to the following questions.

1. Why do you think God made people with different personalities?

   _____

   _____

   _____

2. What type personality would you most like to . . .

   • work for: _____

   _____

   • help you with a project: _____

   _____

   • be friends with: _____

   _____

   • have as a son or daughter: _____

   _____

3. How do you think my (the student's) personality will affect my future?

   _____

   _____

   _____

   _____

   _____
   Parent's Signature

A CALL TO WORSHIP

QuestTruth

Salvation is provided freely to all who repent from sin and accept Jesus Christ by faith. To be "born again" means spiritual birth through the indwelling Holy Spirit that places a believer into the family of God.

UthPstr: Thanks for joining me online—especially Ginny, who is mentoring the girls. We need to talk about the plans for our trip to the Brother Bryan Mission next month. It will be a good opportunity not only for us to help with dinner but to share our faith with others. Have any of you ever tried to witness to another person?

IM4Him: I got to talk to Richard about the Lord. He sits next to me in my world civ class. Anyway, he doesn't believe that faith in Christ is the only way to be saved. I don't really understand his argument, but he believes that all religions have their "great teachers." As long as we are sincere, any religion can lead us into heaven. I didn't know how to answer him, even though I talked about being born again.

PHETI: I've heard people say things like that before. Richard is in my algebra class. He's a nice guy, and I'd like to talk to him. But, like you, I need to know what to say.

UthPstr: I'm sure that Richard is very sincere and that he truly believes what he said. It's important to remember that for centuries mankind has searched for the meaning for our existence. People have tried to find the truth about why we are here and where we go after we die. I want to share an article I recently read—a story that fits. It's a little long, so hang with me.

File Sharing

The story is about a woman who was on a quest. She was determined to learn the meaning of life. In her pursuit of the truth, she attended several prestigious universities. She achieved the highest academic degrees possible. She read every history and philosophy book she could get her hands on and traveled to other countries to meet some famous philosophers.

But at the end of each day, she was no closer to understanding the meaning of life. Her professors did not agree with each other, the books she read presented conflicting information and the philosophers themselves had more questions than answers. But she refused to give up.

During her search she learned of an old monk who she thought could help her. Others hadn't seen him in years, but supposedly he lived in the mountains of Tibet. She packed her bags and began her journey. He was her last hope to understanding the real meaning of life.

After arriving in Tibet, she got directions to a small village three days' journey into the mountains. The mountain passes were so rugged that the trip actually took five days. Exhausted, she finally reached the village. But her quest was not complete. It took two more days, climbing up the steep mountainside, to reach his compound. Although the sun had already set, she saw a light flickering within a hut. She boldly approached the front door and called his name.

"Enter," a voice commanded. When she opened the door, she saw a pleasant-looking gentleman with a book in his hand, sitting at an old wooden desk. "Please come in," he said. "I expected you. How can I help you?"

The woman replied, "I have come on a quest. I must know the meaning of life."

"Please have some tea," the old monk said, so she sat down and took the empty cup from his hand. While the tea was brewing, the woman began to tell all about her search—what she had learned, the important people she had met, and her conclusions. She wanted to make sure that the elderly monk understood her past accomplishments.

The wise old monk patiently listened and listened as he quietly began to pour the tea. She was so engrossed in her own achievements that she didn't notice what he was doing. She continued to talk and he continued to pour. Soon the tea began to spill over the side of the cup and onto her clothes.

"What are you doing!" she yelped. "Can't you see that my cup is full!"

"You're right," he spoke quietly and confidently. "Your cup is full. You are so filled with yourself and your accomplishments that there is nothing more I can say to you. Come back when your cup is empty, and we can talk."

IM4Him: It makes little sense for the woman to travel that far then do all the talking herself. However, I'm not quite sure I understand the connection between Richard's situation and your story, Pastor Scott.

UthPstr: I think we can learn a couple of important lessons from this story. First, it reminds us that people are constantly searching for the meaning to life. Even if it does not involve a long journey like the woman in this story, we still wonder about why we are here. Second, if we're not careful, we can become our own stumbling block to finding the answer. We can become so consumed with ourselves that we will be unable to see the answer—even if it's right in front of our eyes.

2B4Givn: I think I've got it. I recently taught a Bible study on Nicodemus from John 3:1-21. Unlike the woman in your story, Nicodemus was real. But in a similar way he was also searching for the meaning of life. Here's a short version of the lesson.

IM4Him: That's exactly the way Richard thought. He said that Jesus was a good man and teacher—one of many from various religions. I can see how Nicodemus wanted to determine for himself whether Jesus was really from God.

> ### FILE SHARING
>
> As a ruler of the Jews, Nicodemus was a religious leader as well as a political leader. The rabbinical laws guided every Jew in both spiritual and public life. Rabbis were well respected because they represented divine authority on earth. Nicodemus, as a rabbi, was very knowledgeable of Old Testament Scriptures.
>
> His first words revealed the growing conviction shared among the Jewish rulers that Jesus must be a "teacher come from God" (John 3:2). The miracles that Jesus performed proved that God was with Him. Nicodemus wanted to meet this teacher.

2B4Givn: Right! Although interested in the miracles, Nicodemus was searching for something of far greater value. It's possible that Nicodemus' night visit was made in secret to avoid any impression of public support for Jesus or His teachings, or it could have been simply the most convenient time to avoid the crowds.

Immediately upon meeting Jesus, Nicodemus wanted to know if Jesus had really been sent from God. What a shock Nicodemus received! Rather than answer the question, Jesus answered the real question that was on Nicodemus's heart—"Most assuredly, I say to you, unless one is born again, he cannot see the Kingdom of God" (John 3:3).

PHETI: I find it interesting that Jesus began by pointing out Nicodemus's need rather than responding to his question. Jesus knew that what Nicodemus was truly concerned about was his relationship with God, but he had no idea how to enter the Kingdom of God. Nicodemus was searching for the meaning of salvation. That's why Jesus answered the question that was really on Nicodemus' mind.

By the way, I'm curious. How did Richard respond to the words "born again"?

IM4Him: Actually, it was time for the bell so we never got that far. I guess that he'd have no idea what I was talking about.

UthPstr: The idea of being born again didn't make any sense to Nicodemus. He thought Jesus was talking about a physical rebirth. "How can a man be born when he is old? Can he enter a second time into his mother's womb and be born?" (John 3:4). Jesus replied that He wasn't talking about a physical rebirth, but a spiritual one. Jesus explained that the new birth is a work of God through the Holy Spirit (John 3:5-8). "Nicodemus answered and said to Him, 'How can these things be?' " (John 3:9).

2B4Givn: You're right! This was when Jesus asked Nicodemus, "Are you the teacher of Israel and do not know these things?" (John 3:10). Jesus was amazed that a man so educated in the Old Testament did not understand the concept of the new birth. He knew about the law but he missed the promise of grace, which tells us that God loves us in spite of our failures and our sins.

UthPstr: Jesus continued to explain the grace of God, especially the two dramatic differences in the true Kingdom of God from the one that the Jews were expecting. First, it was a spiritual kingdom for those born again by faith. Second was the eventual death of the Messiah. God sent His Son as a sacrifice for the sins of the world. All a person must do is repent of sins and receive Christ.

2B4Givn: We really don't know how Nicodemus responded to that. However, we do know that Nicodemus continued as a ruling Pharisee and at one point defended Jesus against hearsay accusations (John 7:50-51). We also know that after Jesus' crucifixion, Nicodemus brought spices and helped to prepare the body of Jesus for burial (John 19:38-42).

QTee: It looks like Nicodemus was affected by what Jesus said. Otherwise, he wouldn't have defended Jesus or brought spices for Jesus' burial.

UthPstr: You're probably right. But what I want all of you to understand is the similarity between Nicodemus and all people that we have an opportunity to speak to. Like Nicodemus, many things stand in our way in our search for God. For Nicodemus, it was his intellect and background. His faulty understanding of the Old Testament prevented him from understanding the grace of God.

QTee: It seems like intellect and background are also what stood in Richard's way. Are there other things that stand in the way of people coming to know Jesus as their Savior?

UthPstr: Yes, the Samaritan woman in John 4 is another good example. Her obstacle was the magnitude of her sin. She could not understand how God could love someone who had repeatedly committed adultery. Let me remind you of this story.

On His way from Judea to Galilee, Jesus traveled through Samaria. Weary from His journey, Jesus stopped at a well. His disciples continued into the village to buy food. A Samaritan woman came to draw water at the well. Apparently, the woman was an outcast in her own community, because she came alone to the community well. In biblical lands, drawing water while chatting at the well was the social high point of a woman's day. However, this woman had been excluded from village society because of her immoral lifestyle. She was an unmarried woman living openly with the sixth in a series of men.

When Jesus said to her, "Give Me a drink," she was surprised. Before drawing the water, she responded, "How is it that You, being a Jew, ask a drink from me, a Samaritan woman? For Jews have no dealings with Samaritans" (John 4:9).

Jesus began to talk to the woman about God's gift—living water and everlasting life. However, like Nicodemus, she was thinking in practical terms, not about spiritual water that would give her eternal life. "Sir, give me this water, that I may not thirst, nor come here to draw" (John 4:15).

Gr8-1: So, Jesus was using water as a way to teach her spiritual truth? According to John 4:15, it doesn't look like she understood at first.

2B4Givn: She didn't. She had been looking for "real love" in her intimate relations with men. Jesus changed the conversation to focus her attention on her real need—a soul-satisfying drink from the river of life. Her need was spiritual, not physical. She needed to be converted and cleansed from her sin. When Jesus revealed a detailed knowledge of her immorality, she knew Jesus was more than just a Jewish man—"Sir, I perceive that You are a prophet" (John 4:19).

UthPstr: Jesus told her about the grace of God and the need to be cleansed from sin. "God is Spirit," Jesus said, "and those who worship Him must worship in spirit and truth" (John 4:14).

2B4Givn: The woman was amazed at His teaching. It was obvious that she knew something about the Old Testament because she responded, "I know that Messiah is coming. When He comes, He will tell us all things" (John 4:25).

"I who speak to you am He," Jesus responded (John 4:26). The woman was so excited that she ran to tell everyone about Him. Can you imagine what it was like when she entered the village crying, "He told me all that I ever did" (John 4:39)? She wanted to tell others about what He had done in her life.

 UthPstr: According to John 4:42, the testimony of the woman and the ministry of Jesus had a tremendous impact upon the city. "Then they said to the woman, 'Now we believe, not because of what you said, for we ourselves have heard Him and we know that this is indeed the Christ, the Savior of the world.' "

IM4Him: Now I see how Nicodemus and the Samaritan woman were both searching for spiritual birth. But didn't they face different obstacles to their belief? Nicodemus, a religious man, took pride in his position and knowledge of the Old Testament. The woman at the well believed that her sins were too great for God to care about her.

UthPstr: That's right! But notice how Jesus approached each of them differently. In order for Nicodemus to understand God's grace, he had to see himself as a sinner. His religious traditions and knowledge of the Old Testament had convinced him that he was doing everything right. That's why Nicodemus could not understand why Jesus told him that he had to be born again. Jesus patiently helped Nicodemus understand the greatest spiritual truth of the universe—"For God so loved the world that He gave His only begotten Son, that whoever believes in Him should not perish but have everlasting life" (John 3:16).

FACTOID

For a Jewish man to speak to a woman in public—especially a prostitute—was a breach of the rigid social custom. To make matters worse, the woman at the well was a Samaritan—a mixed race whom the Jews despised.

 PHETI: The woman at the well knew she was a sinner. She saw herself as such a terrible sinner that she believed no one could ever really love her.

Samaritans regarded only the Pentateuch (the first five books of Moses) as authoritative. As a result, the rest of the Jews considered them heretics.

2B4Givn: True. Jesus did not focus on her sin, but on what it means to worship God. He told her that she must turn from her life of prostitution and worship God "in spirit and in truth" (John 4:23). He told her that God truly loved her and had provided a way of salvation from her sins.

PHETI: These are really good examples. But I keep thinking about Richard. If we start talking with someone like Richard about the Lord, what should we say?

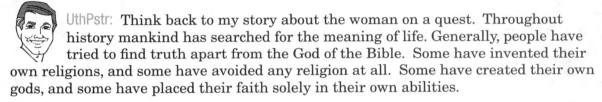

UthPstr: Think back to my story about the woman on a quest. Throughout history mankind has searched for the meaning of life. Generally, people have tried to find truth apart from the God of the Bible. Some have invented their own religions, and some have avoided any religion at all. Some have created their own gods, and some have placed their faith solely in their own abilities.

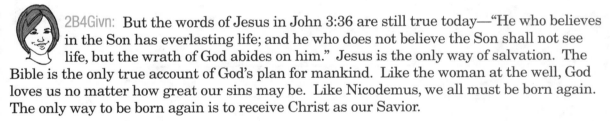

2B4Givn: But the words of Jesus in John 3:36 are still true today—"He who believes in the Son has everlasting life; and he who does not believe the Son shall not see life, but the wrath of God abides on him." Jesus is the only way of salvation. The Bible is the only true account of God's plan for mankind. Like the woman at the well, God loves us no matter how great our sins may be. Like Nicodemus, we all must be born again. The only way to be born again is to receive Christ as our Savior.

UthPstr: Never forget, the meaning of life is found in our personal relationship with Jesus Christ. Keep that in mind as we go to the Mission next month. Oops! Time's up! We'll keep working on some effective ways to talk about Christ in our next meeting. Blessings to all!

John 3 Summary Notes
Follow your teacher's instructions as you summarize each passage.

John 3:1-3

John 3:4-8

John 3:9-13

John 3:14-17

John 3:18-21

John 3:22-36

John 4 Summary Notes Follow your teacher's instructions as you summarize each passage.

John 4:1-6 _____

_____

_____

John 4:7-15 _____

_____

_____

_____

John 4:16-26 _____

_____

_____

John 4:27-38 _____

_____

_____

John 4:39-45 _____

_____

_____

John 4:46-54 _____

_____

_____

_____

The New Birth Complete the assignment in preparation for class discussion.

THE LESSONS

Nicodemus	Samaritan Woman
Describe how he felt about himself.	Describe how she felt about herself.
Describe how he felt about God.	Describe how she felt about God.
What did he believe God required of him?	What did she believe God required of her?
What did Jesus offer him?	What did Jesus offer her?

The grace of God is extended to each of us—
no matter who we are or what we have done.

Nicodemus	Samaritan Woman
How did he respond to God's grace?	How did she respond to God's grace?
_____	_____
_____	_____
_____	_____

THE MESSAGE

1. What is God's goal?

_____

_____

_____

2. What is God's gift to each of us?

_____

_____

_____

3. What is God's attitude toward people?

_____

_____

_____

4. How should man respond to God?

_____

_____

_____

5. How was grace defined?

_____

_____

_____

6. Has God's grace made a difference in you?

_____

_____

_____

Grace says to each of us, "You count." When we accept that grace and experience the new birth, it makes a difference!

Family Chatroom/Sharing the Faith Interact with your parents or another adult and record their responses.

1. Why are many Christians hesitant to share their faith? _____

   _____

   _____

   _____

   _____

   _____

2. What mistakes do some Christians make in talking to others about God?

   _____

   _____

   _____

   _____

   _____

3. Suggest some good ways to talk to others about God.

   _____

   _____

   _____

   _____

   _____

   _____
   Parent's Signature

The Name Above Every Name

Oh what is Jehovah El Shaddai to me?
My Lord, God and Savior, Immanuel, He;
My Prophet, Priest, Sacrifice, Altar and Lamb;
Judge, Advocate, Surety and Witness, I AM;
My Peace and my Life, my Truth and my Way;
My Leader, my Teacher, my Hope and my Stay;
Redeemer and Ransom, Atonement and Friend;
He's Alpha, Omega, Beginning and End.

Yea, more is Jehovah, El Shaddai beside—
Avenger and Shepherd, and Keeper and Guide;
My Horn of Salvation, my Captain in war;
My Dayspring, my Sun, and my Bright Morning Star;
My Wonderful, Counselor, Wisdom and Light;
My Shadow by day, and my Beacon by night;
Pearl, Ornament, Diadem, Treasure untold;
My Strength and my Sun, in Him I behold.

All this is Jehovah Ropheka and more—
My Bread and my Water, my Dwelling, my Door;
My Branch and my Vine, my Lily and Rose;
Rock, Hiding Place, Refuge, Shield, Covert, Repose;
My sure Resurrection, my Glory above;
My King in His beauty, my Bridegroom, my Love;
My all and in all in Christ Jesus I see,
For God hath made Him to be all things to me.

Now say to Thy soul, "What is He to thee?"

–John H. Sammis

DIRECTIONS OF MINISTRY

QUEST TRUTH

Jesus ministered approximately three years through preaching, teaching, and healing as He proclaimed and confirmed the Kingdom of God.

Gr8-1: I really enjoyed our discussion last week about the meaning of life. Thanks for taking the time to meet with us online.

UthPstr: No problem. I enjoyed it too. Your phone message today said that you had some other questions. So, what's up?

Gr8-1: The other day I was telling Tyler about almost getting cut from the basketball team. I wasn't having a very good day because I didn't do well in my science class either. Anyway, we had a discussion in English class yesterday that has me kind of confused.

UthPstr: If it has anything to do with an English assignment, I may not be your best source. I'll sure try any other subject.

Gr8-1: No, this has nothing to do with an English assignment! Someone asked about the meaning of the word "minister." The dictionary says that it is a "clergyman or one who assists in officiating church worship." But a lot of people disagreed. They said that according to 1 Timothy 4:6, it is anyone who shares God's Word with others. You don't have to be paid by a church to be a minister.

UthPstr: Hmm, before we talk about the discussion in English class, give me a little background as to why you're asking this question.

Gr8-1: As I told Tyler, some day I hope to be a doctor. Right now, I'm considering the possibility of becoming a medical missionary. I want to share God's Word with the people I help. Some would say that makes me a "minister," but others disagree.

FACTOID

During Jesus' ministry, He visited over 40 different cities in Palestine, roughly the area now called Israel.

UthPstr: Maybe the best way to answer your question is to begin with a short quiz. What do these two examples have in common?

[This was the third straight day that John had been called to the coach's office for missing a football block. "You have to run the play exactly like it's in the playbook," the coach said. "If you don't learn your blocking assignments, the fullback is going to be sacked every time."]

[Cindy's grade on the last biology experiment was below satisfactory. Although Mr. Taylor had written the steps on the board for conducting the experiment, Cindy thought she could save time by skipping steps 4 and 7. As a result, things didn't turn out like they were supposed to.]

Gr8-1: It looks like they all have something to do with following directions. If John fails his blocking assignments, the running backs probably won't score. If Cindy had not skipped steps 4 and 7, her experiment would have been successful.

UthPstr: You've got the idea. Now, let me ask you a few questions. Do you believe that Jesus gave directions about what His disciples were to say and do? Do you believe that Jesus was following directions when He ministered on earth?

Gr8-1: I'm sure the answer to both of those questions is "yes." I remember your saying that the ministry of Jesus and His disciples helps us to understand what the Lord expects from us.

UthPstr: Thanks for remembering. I'm thinking about how, after His temptation, "Jesus returned to Galilee in the power of the Spirit, and news of Him went out through all the surrounding region. And He taught in their synagogues, being glorified by all" (Luke 4:14-15). This verse tells us that as Jesus began His ministry, people were amazed by His teachings. As a result, no matter where He went, He attracted a crowd.

We don't know how long it was, but Jesus later made a visit to Nazareth, His hometown. Of course, by then everyone had heard about Him, and they were excited to see this boy who had grown up in their town. As a courtesy, the ruler of the synagogue even asked

Jesus to read the Scripture (Luke 4:17). Jesus unrolled the heavy scroll and read from Isaiah (61:1-2), which His listeners knew described the Messiah. Upon completing his reading, Jesus stunned the crowd by saying, "Today this Scripture is fulfilled in your hearing" (Luke 4:21).

Gr8-1: I remember that the crowd was shocked by what He said. Jesus claimed to be the fulfillment of Isaiah's prophecy—that He was actually the promised Messiah.

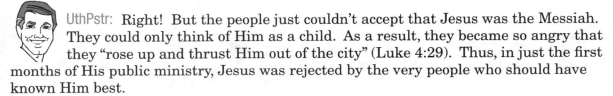

UthPstr: Right! But the people just couldn't accept that Jesus was the Messiah. They could only think of Him as a child. As a result, they became so angry that they "rose up and thrust Him out of the city" (Luke 4:29). Thus, in just the first months of His public ministry, Jesus was rejected by the very people who should have known Him best.

The rejection experienced in Nazareth was repeated over and over throughout the next three years. Finally, the hatred became so great that Jesus was crucified. However, His crucifixion and resurrection were the final proof that He was the Messiah promised in Isaiah 61. Through His crucifixion and resurrection, Jesus completed the task that He described to Nicodemus in John 3:16-17: "For God so loved the world that He gave His only begotten Son, that whoever believes in Him should not perish but have everlasting life. For God did not send His Son into the world to condemn the world, but that the world through Him might be saved."

Sorry to be long-winded in answering your question! I first want to make sure that you understand that God had given clear directions about how Jesus was to conduct His ministry (Matthew 4:23). Even after Jesus left Nazareth, He remained in the countryside of Galilee for many weeks. He continued to preach the gospel. Miracles were performed and many followed and believed in Him. As a result of His popularity, He continued to be met by opposition from the religious leaders. Remember, even though He was following God's directions, He still met opposition.

Gr8-1: How do the disciples fit into all of this? And how does it relate to my question about being a minister?

UthPstr: BPWM—I'm getting there. During His time in Galilee, Jesus chose and trained His followers. After His ministry was completed, the disciples would be responsible to continue His work. He gave them the necessary directions they would need. Throughout His three-year ministry, He trained His disciples for future ministry.

I have a question for you. Where did Jesus do most of His preaching—in the countryside or in cities?

Gr8-1: Most people would say in the countryside. I remember you saying that many people think Jesus was primarily a country preacher because the Sermon on the Mount, the feeding of the 5,000, and many of the miracles did not occur in cities. However, it's very clear from the New Testament that Jesus often visited major cities first.

UthPstr: That's right. During Jesus' day, the area of Palestine was undergoing rapid growth. Its population of around 2.5 to 3 million people lived in numerous cities and towns surrounding Jerusalem. The city of Jerusalem had a population of 60,000 to 90,000. As Jesus carried out His ministry, He focused on the cities throughout Palestine, visiting Jerusalem at least three times.

Gr8-1: I think that by preaching in the cities, Jesus felt He could reach a bigger and more diverse group of people. He not only had the opportunity to preach to large crowds, but He also preached the gospel to various groups such as women, soldiers, religious leaders, the rich, merchants, tax collectors, Gentiles, prostitutes, beggars, the disabled, and the poor.

UthPstr: And Jesus' "city strategy" provided a model for His disciples and the early church, as well as for us today. When He sent the disciples on preaching tours, He directed them toward cities (Matthew 10:5,11-14; Luke 10:1,8-16). They were to preach the gospel wherever they went. By the end of the first century, communities of believers had been established in at least 40 major cities throughout the Roman Empire.

Jesus also had a central message. It was the message of the gospel. Unfortunately, too many people today don't really understand the meaning of the term "gospel." However, Jesus said He came to preach the gospel. He directed His disciples to preach the gospel. Later, He commanded all believers to teach the gospel. So, it's important to know what Jesus meant by the term "gospel."

Gr8-1: I know we call the books of the Bible written by Matthew, Mark, Luke, and John the Gospels. But the word means "good news." I guess that's because the ultimate good news is that Jesus Christ has come as the Messiah, the Savior of the world.

 UthPstr: I'm impressed! Jesus came to save people from sin and restore them to a right relationship with God. This is the Gospel with a capital *G*. In the Book of Romans, Paul explains the need for the gospel in even greater detail by reminding every individual that "There is none righteous, no, not one" (Romans 3:10), and ". . . all have sinned and fall short of the glory of God" (Romans 3:23).

The good news, according to Paul, is that "Christ died for our sins according to the Scriptures, and that He was buried, and that He rose again the third day according to the Scriptures" (1 Corinthians 15:3-4). Thus we have God's promise—"But as many as received Him, to them He gave the right to become the children of God, to those who believe in His name" (John 1:12).

 Gr8-1: But isn't there more to the gospel than just being saved? I see lots of teens who say they're saved. However, they don't walk their talk, if you know what I mean.

 UthPstr: Yes, I do. Jesus' ultimate purpose in the gospel is to create a new group of people who live according to the teachings of God's Word. The gospel does not just address a private relationship with God, but also a public expression of godliness. Accepting the message of the gospel certainly affects our personal life. Even more, it challenges us to look beyond our own self-interests to the interests of others. To believe the gospel is to live no longer for self, but to live for Christ.

Now I want to try to answer the question that you asked earlier. Too many people assume that God's work in the world is accomplished primarily by ordained clergy. The answer to your question is found in Isaiah's prophecy in Isaiah 61. Although Jesus declared that the prophecy of Isaiah 61 was fulfilled in Him, Isaiah described what would happen after the Messiah's initial work was accomplished—"But you shall be named the priests of the Lord; they shall call you the servants of our God" (61:6).

 Gr8-1: Well, priests are ministers. I remember Peter wrote something about the priesthood of believers. Does that mean that all believers are ministers?

UthPstr: Yes! Isaiah declared that the work of ministry would no longer belong exclusively to priests, rabbis, or clergy, but would be done by all of God's people. Just as the Spirit of the Lord had come upon the Lord Jesus Christ, enabling Him to accomplish God's work, so the Spirit would fill and enable Christ's followers to accomplish God's continuing work in the world.

 Gr8-1: That pretty much settles it for me. Whatever career I have in the future, I will still be a minister as I share the gospel and help others. Even now I need to be more serious about my ministry for the Lord. How do I get started?

UthPstr: Although God leads each of us in very different ways, the following facts from my notes are true for every believer.

FILE SHARING

Fact 1—Every follower of Jesus Christ has a responsibility to proclaim the gospel message.

Fact 2—The Spirit of God will enable you to accomplish any task that God has set before you.

Fact 3—Developing a personal relationship with the Lord and living a godly life are not optional—they are requirements.

Fact 4—Serving the Lord is not a future event, but a present reality.

Fact 5—You are responsible to take every opportunity to make Christ known through your words and actions.

 Gr8-1: If I understand you correctly, the way I live my life—on a daily basis—is the first step in my ministry for the Lord.

 UthPstr: That's a good way to put it. Let me tell you a story that I think shows the link between the way we live privately and our ministry publicly.

UthPstr: In April 1999, a high school student had to make a decision that none of us would want to make. A gunman pointed his weapon at this Christian young lady and asked, "Do you believe in God?" She knew that if she answered, "Yes," she would be killed. However, to deny her Lord was unthinkable. So, with what were to be her last words, she calmly answered, "Yes, I believe in God." Look at this article.

FILE SHARING

As the Washington Post reported the story, the two students who shot 13 people did not choose their victims at random. They were acting out of their prejudices. They had deep hostility toward racial minorities and athletes; they also hated Christians. Of the 13 people killed, eight were Christians. Among them was Cassie Bernall. It was Cassie who made the decision not to deny her faith. She had been active in her youth group at Westpool Community Church and was known for carrying a Bible to school. She was in the school library reading her Bible when the two young killers burst in. As her classmate, Mickie Cain, later reported, "She completely stood up for God. When they asked her if there was anyone who had faith in Christ, she spoke up, and they shot her for it."

According to the Boston Globe, on the night of her death, Cassie's brother Chris found a poem Cassie had written just two days prior to her death.

Now I have given up on everything else.
I have found it to be the only way
To really know Christ and to experience
The mighty power that brought
Him back to life again, and to find
Out what it means to suffer and to
Die with him. So, whatever it takes
I will be one who lives in the fresh
Newness of life of those who are
Alive from the dead.

Gr8-1: Wow! What a challenge to us. Thanks, Pastor Scott. I'm going to pray that the Lord gives me the strength to use every opportunity to make Him known through my words and my actions. I know that's the first step in beginning my ministry.

Jesus Shocks His Hearers   Use your Bible and record the answers.

1. According to Luke 4:18-19, Jesus read from a passage in Isaiah 61:1-2. Both passages characterize the Messiah's ministry. Identify these six characteristics.

   1. _____

   2. _____

   3. _____

   4. _____

   5. _____

   6. _____

2. In your own words, restate the following verses in a way that someone might say these statements today.

   ■ "Today this Scripture is fulfilled in your hearing." (Luke 4:21) _____

   _____

   _____

   _____

   ■ "Is this not Joseph's son?" (Luke 4:22) _____

   _____

   _____

   _____

■ "You will surely say this proverb to Me, 'Physician, heal yourself!'" (Luke 4:23)

_____

_____

_____

■ "Assuredly, I say to you, no prophet is accepted in his own country." (Luke 4:24)

_____

_____

_____

3. Why did the people of Nazareth, Jesus' hometown, not believe Him when He made the statement recorded in Luke 4:21?

_____

_____

_____

_____

_____

_____

Family Chatroom   Discuss with your parents their ideas on how teens could serve the Lord.

1. Should Christian teens be concerned about their ministry to the Lord? Why or why not? _____

   _____

   _____

   _____

   _____

2. How would a teen know whether to consider being a full-time minister, missionary, or Christian worker? _____

   _____

   _____

   _____

   _____

3. What are some things a teen could be doing now to minister for the Lord?

   _____

   _____

   _____

   _____

   _____

   _____
   Parent's Signature

JESUS PERFORMS MIRACLES

QuestTruth

Miracles are events that supersede the laws of nature, performed by divine power and for a divine purpose.

QTee: So what did you think of chapel today? I like Spiritual Emphasis Week. It's too bad that the week is almost over.

IM4Him: I agree. The series on "How to Find a Friend I Can Really Trust" has been great. I especially like the quote from Aristotle—"A true friend is one soul in two bodies."

QTee: I like the quote from Henry Ward Beecher the best—"Keep a fair-sized cemetery in your backyard in which to bury the faults of your friends." I need to remember to build my friends up, not tear them down.

IM4Him: That quote made me think of Jennifer and Sandy. They've been friends for years and now they won't even speak to each other. It's all so silly. Just because of a simple misunderstanding, they're now gossiping about each other.

QTee: That's funny you should mention them. When the speaker quoted what Solomon said in Proverbs 19:5—"A false witness will not go unpunished, and he who speaks lies will not escape."—I thought about them too.

IM4Him: He was exactly right. Although a friend's betrayal is terrible and wrong, it has happened for centuries. Like he said, Jesus was betrayed by Judas Iscariot for 30 pieces of silver. But I never thought about other people who betrayed Him—people who should have been His friends.

QTee: You mean, like the Pharisees? There was the time that Jesus went to Levi's house for dinner (Matthew 9:10-11 and Luke 5:29-31). He was the tax collector who followed the Lord. According to Matthew's Gospel, "many tax collectors and sinners came and sat down with Him and His disciples. And when the Pharisees saw it, they asked His disciples, 'Why does your Teacher eat with tax collectors and sinners?' "

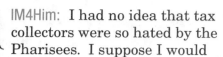

IM4Him: I had no idea that tax collectors were so hated by the Pharisees. I suppose I would be angry too if the tax collectors were keeping some of the money for themselves and only giving part of it as a tax to Rome. The Pharisees thought they were thieves and traitors to the Jewish nation.

QTee: Still, the Pharisees were wrong to attack Jesus. Jesus knew they were self-righteous hypocrites when He said, "Those who are well have no need of a physician, but those who are sick. But go and learn what this means: I desire mercy and not sacrifice."

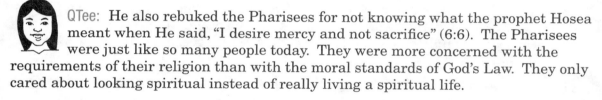

IM4Him: It's obvious that the Pharisees considered themselves religiously "well"—that is, pure and righteous. The tax collectors and sinners knew they were sinners. That's why Jesus pointed out that salvation can only come to those who really know they need it.

QTee: He also rebuked the Pharisees for not knowing what the prophet Hosea meant when He said, "I desire mercy and not sacrifice" (6:6). The Pharisees were just like so many people today. They were more concerned with the requirements of their religion than with the moral standards of God's Law. They only cared about looking spiritual instead of really living a spiritual life.

IM4Him: I keep thinking about what we heard today. I can't believe how much Jesus and His disciples were criticized. Even the disciples of John the Baptist didn't seem to understand that the Messiah was there. They said, "Why do we and the Pharisees fast often, but Your disciples do not fast?"

QTee: Even when He performed miracles, people criticized Him. It's interesting how Jesus used the wedding party illustration. Because a wedding is a time for joy and celebration, you don't spend your time in prayer and fasting. Jesus was only going to be with them for a short time. After He was gone, there would be plenty of time for prayer and fasting.

IM4Him: Yeah, it's not like He was performing miracles to gain attention, to collect money or to make Himself famous. Instead, Jesus often told those who saw a miracle to "tell no one" about it. He didn't want people to come to Him because they wanted to see a magic show.

QTee: It seems like the people who should have been Jesus' friends were the ones who criticized Him the most. It began when He read the Scriptures in the synagogue in His own town. From that point until He was nailed to the cross, He was criticized and rejected.

 IM4Him: It really does hurt when people—especially your friends—criticize and lie about you. Just imagine what it was like for Jesus when He knew He would be betrayed by one of His own disciples. Because of what He went through, He can understand our pain when our friends betray us.

 QTee: Just like so many other people, I seem to only think of Jesus as my Savior—as the one who provides the ticket to heaven. I keep forgetting that He is just as interested in my life right now as He is in my eternal life. It really hit me when the speaker talked about the "Ultimate Test of Friendship."

 IM4Him: I remember John 15:12-17 where Jesus said, "This is my commandment, that you love one another as I have loved you. Greater love has no one than this, than to lay down one's life for his friends." And then He said, a few verses later, "I have called you friends."

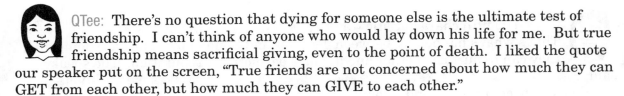 QTee: There's no question that dying for someone else is the ultimate test of friendship. I can't think of anyone who would lay down his life for me. But true friendship means sacrificial giving, even to the point of death. I liked the quote our speaker put on the screen, "True friends are not concerned about how much they can GET from each other, but how much they can GIVE to each other."

 IM4Him: Since Jennifer and Sandy are our friends, maybe we need to try to help them get over their differences. We could use the checklist the speaker gave us. Do you have your list, "Characteristics of a True Friend"?

 QTee: Yes, I have it here. The first characteristic I wrote down is "A true friend shares your values and makes wise decisions."

 IM4Him: It's like our speaker said, Amos 3:3 asked a very important question: "Can two walk together, unless they are agreed?" The close friends we choose need to hold the same beliefs that we hold. Otherwise, we'll have conflict and one of us will have to compromise.

QTee: Here's the second characteristic: "A true friend doesn't pretend to be perfect." I really liked that one! So many times, people act so phony. They pretend that they never have any problems. A true friend is not afraid to admit that they've faced difficulties. Rather than gloat about the problems you are facing, a true friend tries to encourage you through difficult times.

IM4Him: For the third characteristic, I wrote "A true friend practices confidentiality." That's a biggie for me. I can't stand it when "friends" talk behind my back. They just need to keep quiet.

QTee: And the speaker also asked us if we've ever talked behind the back of one of our friends. Unfortunately, my answer was "Yes." He was exactly right. Before we can expect confidentiality from our friends, we need to learn to keep secrets ourselves. People who share secrets about others can't be trusted.

IM4Him: The next characteristic he gave was "A true friend accepts you for who you are." His illustration was true about friends who get mad at you because they don't agree with you. If you are trying to impress someone just to make a friend, you're traveling down a dangerous road. Once you give up your individuality, you will always be a slave to what your "friend" thinks you should be.

QTee: His fifth characteristic was "A true friend never seeks to harm you." That's what's happening between Jennifer and Sandy now. They are doing all they can to hurt each other and damage each other's reputation. The speaker said, "True friends always try to make each other successful." Makes me question whether I've been a good friend lately!

IM4Him: I like what the speaker said at the end of chapel about friendships being fragile. Having broken one of my mom's best cups, I could relate when he said, "Friendships need to be treated as carefully as we would pick up an expensive piece of china. We should never take friendships for granted or treat them carelessly. True friends are difficult to find. And once found, they should be cherished for a lifetime."

QTee: It's no wonder that Jesus uses the word "friend" to describe what it means to really love one another—"This is My commandment, that you love one another as I have loved you. Greater love has no one than this, than to lay down one's life for his friends" (John 15:12-17).

IM4Him: Jesus demonstrates all of the characteristics of being a true friend. He will never betray, embarrass or lie about us. He is a friend who will never leave us, no matter how difficult things may get.

 QTee: I'll call Jennifer if you'll call Sandy. We really want the best for them. Maybe we can all get together and talk about being friends. It would be nice to put all that mess behind us.

 IM4Him: I agree. By the way, here's a quote I really like. SYL

FILE SHARING

"Love One Another As I Have Loved You!"

"Love one another as I have loved you"
May seem impossible to do—
But if you will try to trust and believe
Great are the joys that you will receive . . .
For love makes us patient, understanding and kind,
and we judge with our hearts and not with our mind . . .
For as soon as love enters the heart's open door,
the faults we once saw are not there anymore,
and the things that seemed wrong begin to look right
When viewed in the softness of love's gentle light . . .
For love works in ways that are wondrous and strange,
And there is nothing in life that love cannot change,
And all that God promised will some day come true
When you love one another the way He loves You.

–Helen Steiner Rice

Moments of Miracles/Part 1
In each section, write the miracles that correspond with the Scriptures.

	Matthew	Mark	Luke	John
1.				2:7
2.				4:50
3.		1:25	4:35	
4.			5:5	
5.	8:15	1:31	4:39	
6.	8:3	1:41	5:12	
7.	9:2	2:5	5:20	
8.	12:13	3:5	6:6	
9.	8:13		7:10	
10.			7:14	
11.	8:26	4:39	8:24	
12.	8:32	5:8	8:33	
13.	9:22	5:29	8:44	
14.	9:25	5:41	8:54	
15.	9:29			
16.	9:33			
17.			5:8	
18.	14:19	6:41	9:16	6:11

	Matthew	Mark	Luke	John
19.	14:25	6:48		6:19
20.	15:28	7:29		
21.		7:34		
22.	15:36	8:6		
23.		8:25		
24.				9:7
25.	17:18	9:25	9:42	
26.	17:27			
27.	12:22	11:4		
28.			13:10	
29.			14:4	
30.			17:11	
31.				11:43
32.	20:30	10:46	18:35	
33.	21:19	11:14		
34.	26:51	14:47	22:50	18:10
35.	28:6	16:6	24:6	20:9
36.				21:6

Moments of Miracles/Part 2   Summarize your study of Jesus' miracles as part of class discussion.

1. Define "miracles." _____

_____

_____

2. Why did Jesus perform miracles?

- _____

- _____

- _____

- _____

3. Why did Jesus <u>not</u> perform some miracles?

- _____

- _____

- _____

4. Over what five areas do Jesus' miracles demonstrate power?

1) _____

2) _____

3) _____

4) _____

5) _____

5. About one-third of Jesus' miracles were related to people with disabilities. What should be our attitude toward those who are different from ourselves?

_____

_____

_____

6. What are the three miracles recorded by all four Gospel writers?

1) _____

2) _____

3) _____

7. There are areas of controversy concerning miracles. How would you answer each statement?

1) Miracles are not possible—the stories are just myths! _____

_____

_____

_____

2) Miracles don't happen today. _____

_____

_____

_____

3) Life itself should be considered a miracle. _____

_____

_____

Family Chatroom/"Miracles" Today

Interact with your parents or another adult mentor and record their responses.

1. Why did Jesus perform miracles while He was on earth? _____

   _____

   _____

   _____

2. Why are similar miracles not a common occurrence in our churches today?

   _____

   _____

   _____

3. Has there ever been an event in our family in which God especially intervened (a "miracle") for our benefit? If so, describe one.

   _____

   _____

   _____

4. What daily experiences should be considered miracles? _____

   _____

   _____

   _____

   _____
   Parent's Signature

THE BEGINNING OF CONFLICTS

QuestTruth

Jesus declared the Sabbath a day for doing what is needful and helpful. Early Christians established the first day of the week as a day of worship and rest.

 IM4Him: It felt good to get together for pizza last night. It's been a while since our whole family's been together and just talked.

 2B4Givn: I couldn't have come if I hadn't just finished my midterm exams. It was a good break before starting the second half of the semester.

 IM4Him: You know, it's not often that Dad talks about some of the conversations he has at work—probably because of doctor-patient confidentiality. Even last night he never used any names or any specific facts.

 2B4Givn: Yeah, I know. I've sure been thinking a lot about what he said. I can understand why his patient was so upset. I'd be angry too if my spouse lied to me and couldn't be trusted.

 IM4Him: Dad was right. Being honest is really tough. He made his point when he asked if we had ever said something we really didn't mean like . . .

- I'd like to get together with you sometime.
- You look like you've lost weight.
- I really like what you're wearing.
- Don't worry, you didn't hurt my feelings.

2B4Givn: Like Dad said, consistently telling the truth is one of the hardest things a person does. It's because none of us likes conflict. Sometimes, even when you tell the truth in the most loving and compassionate way, you cannot avoid conflict. Rather than upset people, we just avoid conflict by shading the truth. All the time we know that we are really telling a lie. This not only causes serious problems in our relationships with others, but it also damages our own integrity.

Like Dad said, that's why telling the truth is included as one of the Ten Commandments. God knew that our tendency would be to avoid the truth and to lie. Therefore, He made it very clear that we are not to give false witness.

IM4Him: Our discussion helped me to better understand what Mr. Gifford said today in Bible class. He gave us several examples of how Jesus spoke the truth and how that led to conflict. For example, Jesus made it clear that mankind was sinful and needed to be born again. When the religious leaders misinterpreted the Scriptures, Jesus pointed out their error.

 2B4Givn: Most of the conflict Jesus had was with the religious leaders—the Pharisees. This name comes from a word meaning separated. This religious movement began approximately 200 years before the time of Christ. The Pharisees were very concerned that every tiny aspect of the Law of Moses was kept.

 IM4Him: I remember reading about how the Pharisees emphasized the keeping of the oral law. Mr. Gifford said that the oral law included a vast number of interpretations and explanations of the Old Testament. It was passed down from one generation of priests to the next.

 2B4Givn: Right. Over the years, as the oral law continued to grow, it became focused on trifling details. For example, the command not to work on the Sabbath was expanded and illustrated with hundreds of explanations and exceptions. According to oral law, a person was allowed to spit on rocky ground on the Sabbath but not on soft or dusty ground. Spitting on soft or dusty ground might move the dirt, which in the Pharisees' eyes, meant the person was plowing or watering plants!

So, it is not surprising to find Jesus in conflict with the Pharisees about the purpose of the Sabbath. The meaning of God's Fourth Commandment, "Remember the Sabbath day to keep it holy," was changed dramatically by the oral traditions of the Pharisees.

 IM4Him: According to Mr. Gifford, in Matthew 12:1-8, Jesus' disciples were hungry and began to pluck heads of grain to eat. The only problem was, they did it on the Sabbath. When the Pharisees saw what the disciples did, they complained to Jesus and said, "Look, Your disciples are doing what is not lawful to do on the Sabbath!" (Matthew 12:2).

 2B4Givn: Actually, there was no law against picking grain in order to eat on the Sabbath (Deuteronomy 23:15). What was prohibited was labor that made a profit. Farmers could not harvest grain to make money, but a person could gather enough grain to feed himself.

IM4Him: Dad said that the Pharisees were determined to oppose Jesus in every way they could. He referred to Matthew 12 and how the Sabbath laws do not restrict deeds of necessity (verses 3-4), service to God (verses 5-6) or acts of mercy (verses 7-8). Jesus reminded the Pharisees that the Sabbath was made for man's benefit and God's glory. The Sabbath laws were not meant to make people miserable.

 2B4Givn: For sure, what Jesus said angered the Pharisees. All of Israel looked to them to interpret the Law and the Scriptures. Yet, in just a few sentences, Jesus told them that what they were doing and teaching was all wrong.

 IM4Him: Yes, and He didn't stop there. In verse 8 He said, "For the Son of Man is Lord even of the Sabbath." This was an undeniable statement to His deity. Jesus not only claimed authority over their Sabbath laws, but, as Creator, over the Sabbath itself.

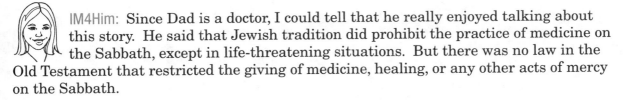 2B4Givn: On the following Sabbath, Jesus went into the synagogue. The Pharisees wondered what He would do next. Within minutes, Jesus saw a man with a withered hand and healed him. Immediately, the Pharisees accused Him, saying it was illegal to heal on the Sabbath (Matthew 12:10).

 IM4Him: Since Dad is a doctor, I could tell that he really enjoyed talking about this story. He said that Jewish tradition did prohibit the practice of medicine on the Sabbath, except in life-threatening situations. But there was no law in the Old Testament that restricted the giving of medicine, healing, or any other acts of mercy on the Sabbath.

2B4Givn: That's why Jesus reminded them in verse 12, ". . . it is lawful to do good on the Sabbath." Of course, the reaction of the Pharisees to Jesus' teaching about the Sabbath was predictable—they were furious! It's just like Dad said—the man was glad, Jesus was sad, and the Pharisees were mad. The Pharisees were so angry that they "went out and plotted against Him, how they might destroy Him" (Matthew 12:14).

FACTOID

The Pharisees feared Jesus as much as they hated Him. They were concerned that His popularity might have political repercussions, drawing Roman troops to the area and causing the loss of what little independence the Jews had.

 IM4Him: The conflict between Jesus and the Pharisees had become very personal. Their hatred for Him was so strong that no matter what Jesus said, they would not listen to Him.

2B4Givn: That was a message that Dad really wanted us to understand last night—unresolved conflict becomes personal. When it becomes personal, emotions get in the way of reason.

 IM4Him: That's exactly what happened between the Pharisees and Jesus. It was not long before Jesus encountered another group of Pharisees. These Pharisees continued to try to trap the Lord by showing the multitudes that He was disobeying the Law.

 2B4Givn: According to Matthew 12:22, one of the Pharisees brought a demon-possessed, blind and mute man to Jesus. When Jesus healed the man, the multitudes were amazed and said, "Could this be the Son of David?" But the Pharisees responded, "This fellow does not cast out demons except by Beelzebub, the ruler of the demons" (Matthew 12:24). Of course, the Pharisees were implying that Jesus was from Satan, the exact opposite of the truth.

Knowing their thoughts, Jesus replied by showing how illogical their accusation was— "If Satan casts out Satan, he is divided against himself. How then will his kingdom stand?" (Matthew 12:26).

 IM4Him: It's hard to believe that anyone could become that angry. But I've seen it happen. I've seen people totally lose it.

 2B4Givn: Me too. But the accusation against Jesus was more than just illogical. It was the worst type of blasphemy. For the first time in history God's Son, standing among them as a Man, performed obvious miracles by the power of God's Holy Spirit. Not only did they deny that Jesus was the Son of God, they attributed the power of God's Holy Spirit to Satan.

 IM4Him: It's no wonder that Jesus proclaimed, "Anyone who speaks a word against the Son of Man, it will be forgiven him; but whoever speaks against the Holy Spirit, it will not be forgiven him, either in this age or in the age to come" (Matthew 12:32).

 2B4Givn: It's like Dad said, the Pharisees had already made their choice. Jesus presented the truth and they chose to deny it. In spite of all of the evidence that Jesus Himself presented, they were committed to oppose Him. Although Jesus was in constant conflict with the religious leaders, He didn't compromise the truth.

IM4Him: I really liked Dad's list of personality types who fail to tell the truth.

- The CHEATER lies to get an advantage over someone else.
- The PRETENDER lies to make himself look better than someone else.
- The MANIPULATOR lies to control a situation or someone else.
- The SLANDERER lies to hurt others.
- The EXAGGERATOR lies to get attention.
- The PROMISE BREAKER lies for personal convenience.

2B4Givn: It seems like I know people who fit every one of those personality types. And Dad was right, our relationships are affected when we lie. When we lie, we reflect the personality of Satan rather than the image of God, just like John said in 8:44-45, "You are of your father the devil, and the desires of your father you want to do. He was a murderer from the beginning, and does not stand in the truth, because there is no truth in him. When he speaks a lie, he speaks from his own resources, for he is a liar and the father of it."

IM4Him: Also, when we lie, we hurt other people and consequently destroy our relationship with them. That's why Paul says in 1 Corinthians 13:6 that love "does not rejoice in iniquity, but rejoices in the truth." And he goes on to say in Ephesians 4:25, "Therefore, putting away lying, 'Let each one speak truth with his neighbor,' for we are members of one another." The only way to maintain good relationships with others is to tell the truth.

2B4Givn: Remember that Dad said many people end up coming to see him as a result of being untruthful. I think that's why he wanted to be so clear with us. He didn't want us to damage our relationships with others by not telling the truth. His advice on telling the truth was so practical. I put it in my personal journal so I would remember. Let me share these three important points with you.

FILE SHARING

1. **You must tell the truth at all times.** It's just like Proverbs 11:3 states, "The integrity of the upright will guide them, but the perversity of the unfaithful will destroy them." It does no good to tell the truth in some instances and avoid the truth in others. Unless you are known as a consistent truth-teller, you will gain the reputation of being a liar and, therefore, an untrustworthy person.

2. You must tell the whole truth.
Matthew 5:37 states, "But let your 'Yes' be 'Yes,' and your 'No,' 'No.' For whatever is more than these is from the evil one." There is always the temptation to tell just enough of the truth to keep you out of trouble. Proverbs 10:10 reminds us that when the truth is held back, there will be trouble. On the other hand, you must also be careful to not say more than the actual truth. This happens when a person adds opinions, interpretations, or spins the story to someone's advantage.

3. You must tell the truth in love. *Sometimes the truth does hurt. Especially when it is aimed at someone else. The truth should not be told with the intent to hurt others. Proverbs 12:18 states, "There is one who speaks like the piercings of a sword, but the tongue of the wise promotes health." In other words, there are some who use words to hurt people and others who use words to bring healing.*

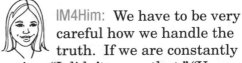

IM4Him: We have to be very careful how we handle the truth. If we are constantly saying, "I didn't mean that," "You misunderstood me," or "That's not really what I meant," then that's a good sign we're using words carelessly.

2B4Givn: Yeah. The words we use can hurt or heal. They can destroy relationships or strengthen them. Words can either cause others to question our integrity or cause them to trust us.

IM4Him: Last night's conversation, and today's Bible class, have really given me a lot to think about. I want to make sure that the words I use reflect the true me. Thanks for your help.

FACTOID

The word true comes from an Old English word *trewe*. From this word we get both the words truth and trust. Thus, the words are intricately related, both in origin and practice. Trust is based on truth. Human relationships are most often destroyed when one or more people are involved in deception. Eventually, the truth is known but the bonds of trust are broken. To earn trust, you must tell the truth.

QuestFile 11.1

The Sabbath Record your answers as your class discusses the Sabbath.

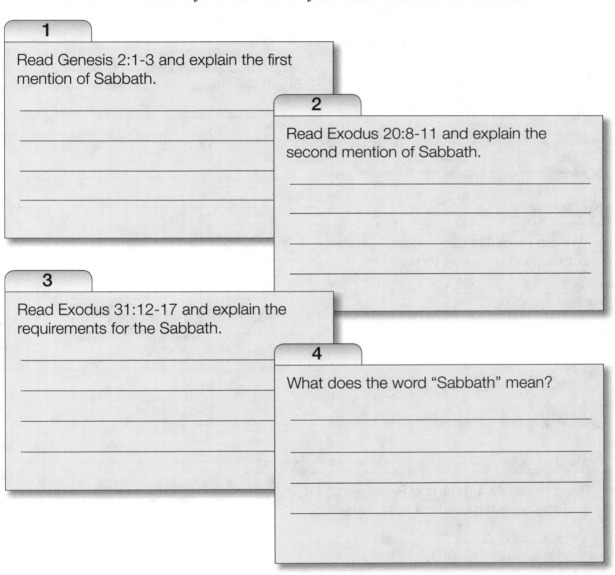

1

Read Genesis 2:1-3 and explain the first mention of Sabbath.

_____

_____

_____

_____

2

Read Exodus 20:8-11 and explain the second mention of Sabbath.

_____

_____

_____

_____

3

Read Exodus 31:12-17 and explain the requirements for the Sabbath.

_____

_____

_____

4

What does the word "Sabbath" mean?

_____

_____

_____

_____

5

If Jesus did not violate these Commandments, why were the Pharisees so furious with Him?

_____

_____

_____

6

What did Jesus mean when He said that the Sabbath was made for man?

_____

_____

_____

_____

7

Why do most Christians not observe the Sabbath on Saturday today?

_____

_____

_____

_____

8

Read Isaiah 58:13-14 and state the principles for observing the Sabbath.

_____

_____

_____

_____

9

Read Hebrews 4:9-11 and Revelation 14:13, and explain what our final Sabbath will be.

_____

_____

_____

_____

QuestFile 11.2

Sabbath Rest Today Discuss with your parents how your family feels toward a day set apart each week for the Lord.

1. What practices from the Old Testament Sabbath should Christians observe on the Lord's Day?

_____

_____

2. What do parents, or grandparents, remember about how differently the Lord's Day was observed in the past?

_____

_____

3. If a family member must work on Sunday, what other ways could a Sabbath rest be observed?

_____

_____

4. How could a family observe the principles of Isaiah 58:13-14? *"If you turn away your foot from the Sabbath, from doing your pleasure on My holy day, and call the Sabbath a delight, the holy day of the Lord honorable, and shall honor Him, not doing your own ways, nor finding your own pleasure, nor speaking your own words, then you shall delight yourself in the Lord; and I will cause you to ride on the high hills of the earth, and feed you with the heritage of Jacob your father. The mouth of the Lord has spoken."*

_____

_____

_____
Parent's Signature

Telling the Truth Summary Notes
Summarize what you have learned regarding telling the truth.

Why is telling the truth such an important principle of life? _____

_____

_____

How does lying destroy trust between people in a relationship? _____

_____

_____

What motivates people to lie? _____

_____

_____

Why do truth-tellers often face conflicts? _____

_____

_____

What biblical commands regarding truth-telling are important? _____

_____

_____

What personal lessons can you apply to your life? _____

_____

_____

SERMON ON THE MOUNT

QUEST TRUTH

While Jesus fulfilled all the Old Testament Law and prophecy, He taught that the Kingdom of God demanded a higher standard of righteousness as believers sought to live by the Spirit toward God and in love toward one another.

Gr8-1: Hey everybody! I think I've found a great story that we might want to use in our presentation. See what you think.

FILE SHARING

Man in Old West tried for stealing horse *(It's important to know that stealing a horse in the Old West was a very grave and serious offense. A person could be hanged if found guilty of such an action.)*

It so happened that the man whose horse was stolen had always made it a point to get the best of any person with whom he had any business. He had never tried to do anything good for anyone other than himself. Consequently, he didn't have a single friend in the entire town.

The case was tried and presented to the jury. The evidence against the accused man was pretty strong. After about 30 minutes of deliberation, the jury returned to the courtroom and the foreman read the verdict: "We find the defendant not guilty if he will return the horse."

After the judge silenced the laughter in the courtroom, he admonished the jury, "I cannot accept that verdict. You will have to return to your deliberations until you reach another verdict."

The jury went back into their room to decide another verdict. No member of the jury had any particular liking for the man whose horse had been stolen. At one time or another he had taken advantage of each of them. About an hour passed before the jury could reach another verdict. They re-entered the courtroom. They took their place in the jury box and the courtroom grew silent.

"Gentlemen of the jury," began the judge, "have you reached a verdict?" The foreman of the jury stood up and replied, "Yes we have, your honor." "What is your verdict?" asked the judge.

The courtroom was totally silent. You could have heard a pin drop. Everyone eagerly awaited the verdict. The foreman read the decision reached by the "twelve good men, tried and true."

"We find the defendant NOT guilty, and he can KEEP the horse!"

The courtroom exploded with laughter!

QTee: What a funny story! I really like it. I also think it fits with what Jesus taught in the Sermon on the Mount. If you spend your life trying to take advantage of others, never caring about them in any way except what you can get from them or what they can do for you, you will end up a loser, like the man whose horse was stolen.

PHETI: The bottom line is: If you want to have a friend, then be a friend. If you want other people to help you, then help other people. If you want justice from others, then practice justice toward them. Regardless of what you may think, we do reap what we sow (Galatians 6:7).

QTee: That's great! We've got to work that into our presentation. It's funny that it never occurred to me, but the longest sermon Jesus ever preached was the Sermon on the Mount (Matthew 5–7). And, as Mr. Gifford explained, it is the most complete explanation of how we should live as Christians—especially in our relationships to one another.

PHETI: That's why I'm so glad we were assigned this topic. Not only is there a lot of information available, it's also very interesting. So, what do we do next?

Gr8-1: Let's begin by reviewing our research on the Sermon on the Mount. One of the things I learned is how Jesus provided the moral principles upon which believers are to live (Matthew 5:1-16). The remainder of the sermon (chapters 6 and 7) is devoted to explaining how these moral principles are to be applied. Jesus not only gave us the principles for living, but also showed us some practical examples.

PHETI: I learned that the Sermon on the Mount is related to the Old Testament Law and the prophets. Jesus said in Matthew 5:17, "Do not think that I came to destroy the Law or the Prophets. I did not come to destroy but to fulfill." What Jesus taught in the Sermon on the Mount was not meant to replace the moral teaching of the Old Testament. Instead, He emphasized that they formed only the baseline. To be true believers, we must "exceed expectations."

QTee: The Matthew 5:17 passage helps in understanding the conflict between Jesus and the Pharisees about the observance of the Sabbath. As a result of the many oral traditions of the Sabbath, its true meaning had been forgotten. The Pharisees' interpretation of God's commandment had actually replaced the commandment itself. Jesus had to remind them of what God had actually said. But they reacted by accusing Jesus of destroying the Sabbath.

> **FACTOID**
>
> The Sermon on the Mount was probably given near the city of Capernaum on the northern coast of the Sea of Galilee. More than half the Lord's teaching and miracles occurred near the Sea of Galilee.

Gr8-1: It seems that the entire focus of the Sermon on the Mount is to explain what the Law really means. After stating the moral principles in the first 16 verses of chapter 5, Jesus reviewed the Old Testament teaching on murder, adultery, divorce, oaths, retaliation, love, charitable deeds, prayer, fasting, and wealth. Each time, He began by stating what the Old Testament taught on these subjects and then explained what God really intended—not just the letter of the law but the spirit behind it.

QTee: But, like Mr. Gifford said in class, pointing out the error of the Pharisees and other religious leaders was not the only focus of the Sermon on the Mount. Jesus was also interested in describing a new lifestyle that was to be adopted by all those who followed Him. The religious lifestyle of the Pharisees did not honor God. In Jesus' sermon He explained that ". . . unless your righteousness exceeds the righteousness of the scribes and Pharisees, you will by no means enter the kingdom of heaven" (Matthew 5:20).

PHETI: All of that sounds good. I've been making notes on how we can actually make the presentation. I've got a lot in PowerPoint already. By the way, did you do your research on the Beatitudes like we decided?

Gr8-1: Sure I did! Here's what I've learned so far. The Sermon on the Mount begins with a series of "blessed are" statements known as the Beatitudes (Matthew 5:3-10). The word "blessed" in these verses refers to being happy. The Beatitudes contrast the world's idea of happiness with true happiness.

QTee: That fits with my research. In the eyes of the world, happiness is found in riches, having a good time, having lots of "stuff," and so on. The real truth is that true happiness is not related to these things. True happiness comes when we live by the values God has set in His Word.

PHETI: That's good. Now, I've got an idea for how to structure that part of our presentation. After Jesus gave the Beatitudes, He turned His attention to the Old Testament Law. Reminding His hearers that His teaching did not contradict the Law, He began to explain the true meaning of what God said. He did this by selecting a number of case histories from the Law and then explaining how the Law was to be fulfilled. We could use these case histories as kind of an outline for our presentation.

Gr8-1: Sounds good to me. I think I have an example of what you're talking about. When Jesus talked about murder, He reminded His hearers that the law forbids murder, but then He went on to say that the root of murder grows from anger and hatred. Rather than letting anger continue to grow, the true believer must try to make peace—even if the other person is at fault! He must take the first step to be reconciled to his brother. That's why John wrote, "whoever hates his brother is a murderer, and you know that no murderer has eternal life abiding in him" (1 John 3:15).

QTee: Here's another example. In Matthew 5:27-30 Jesus pointed out that adultery is more than committing a sexual sin. Adultery occurs when a person commits lust in his or her heart. He illustrated how terrible lust is when He said in verse 29, "If your right eye causes you to sin, pluck it out and cast it from you; for it is more profitable for you that one of your members perish, than for your whole body to be cast into hell."

Gr8-1: Obviously, Jesus was not advocating self-mutilation. Actually, plucking out your eye would not cure lust, because lust is an attitude of the heart. He was using this graphic hyperbole to illustrate the seriousness of sins and evil desire. The point is, it would be more profitable to lose a part of the body than to bear the eternal consequences of the guilt from such a sin. Sin must be dealt with drastically before it destroys us.

PHETI: You sound like a preacher already! But I agree. If you take a look at all of the case histories Jesus gave, you'll see that the problem really is the heart. I learned that the Pharisees focused on rules and regulations; Jesus focused on the attitude of the heart.

Gr8-1: According to my research, Jesus gave the Sermon on the Mount to His followers to help them understand how they should live in His Kingdom (Matthew 6–7). In these two chapters, Jesus provided four guidelines for those who seek to follow Him. I think that these guidelines should be included in our presentation. However, you guys need to add some explanation for each one.

Guideline 1: *We should seek to please God, who sees in secret, rather than men, who judge by outward actions.* (Matthew 6:5-6)

QTee: Okay, I'll try first. I think it's natural for us to want to be respected as a follower of God. But there are many religious games that draw people away from the reality of God's Kingdom. In Jesus' day, one game was to have a trumpeter announce when someone was going to give alms (an offering) to the poor. Although the poor would come, so would the observers. As a result, everyone could see the generosity and compassion of the giver. Jesus said these actions were worthless because they weren't done from the heart.

PHETI: Another common game was played with prayer. When a man wanted to pray, he would go to a busy street corner or a crowded synagogue and stand to pray aloud. Often he would pray very wordy, long prayers in an attempt to make others think that he was holy. Even when men took a vow to go without food, they would be sure to look like they were in pain so that everyone would feel sorry for them. Again, their actions were for show, not from the heart.

Gr8-1: We're on the right track. Jesus described His true followers as those who did not play religious games. They were not concerned with pleasing men. They only wanted to please God. Here's the second one. See what you think.

Guideline 2: *We are to trust God completely to meet our needs.*

(Matthew 6:19-33)

PHETI: Okay, me first on this one. In Jesus' day even the disciples believed that wealth was a sign of God's blessing. Thus, a rich man was viewed as being blessed by God, while a poor man was out of favor with God. That's why Jesus said, "Do not lay up for yourselves treasures on earth . . ." (verse 19).

Gr8-1: Right! Jesus warned against determining our spirituality based upon our possessions. As His followers, we are not to spend all our time and energy focused on becoming rich and gaining material possessions. Whether we have much or little, our relationship with Him is an attitude of the heart. Okay, let's try the next one.

Guideline 3: *We are to express trust in God through prayer and our complete dependence upon Him.* (Matthew 7:7-11)

QTee: I've got it. Jesus reminds us that we are to approach life with a deep sense of our need for God's good gifts. That's why Jesus said, "Ask, and it will be given to you . . ." (7:7). We are not only to realize our dependence upon Him in everything, but also realize that He will supply us with all we need."

Gr8-1: It's fun doing this together. I'll take the last one. Jesus concluded His sermon by challenging us to make a decision. We stand at a crossroad—Jesus' way or the way of the world. We can either choose to obey His words and follow Him, or we can ignore His words and go another direction. The bottom line is . . .

Guideline 4: *We are to obey the words of Jesus.* (Matthew 7:24-27)

QTee: These are all really good! Now I'm beginning to understand why Mr. Gifford said that maintaining good relationships is like putting up Christmas lights. They are easily tangled, hard to unravel, and then you never really know if they're going to work. However, when they do, there's nothing better.

Gr8-1: The best thing that we can bring to a relationship is a godly attitude, just like Jesus described in the Sermon on the Mount. Check out my notes.

FILE SHARING

- Treat others as you would want them to treat you. (7:12)

- Don't be judgmental or critical of others. (7:1)

- Love others, even when they curse you. (5:44)

- Don't retaliate; instead, turn the other cheek. (5:39)

- Avoid anger and seek to forgive those who hurt you. (5:22-24)

PHETI: That's a good summary. We have lots of material for our presentation. Let's meet after school tomorrow and finish our outline. See you then!

The Beatitudes/Matthew 5:3-10 Summarize each characteristic based on class discussion.

PRINCIPLE
Blessed are the poor in spirit.

PRODUCT
Theirs is the kingdom of heaven.

PRACTICE

PRESCRIPTION

PERSONAL APPLICATION

PRINCIPLE
Blessed are those who mourn.

PRODUCT
They shall be comforted.

PRACTICE

PRESCRIPTION

PERSONAL APPLICATION

Blessed are the meek.

They shall inherit the earth.

_____

_____

_____

_____

_____

_____

_____

_____

_____

Blessed are those who hunger and thirst for righteousness.

They shall be filled.

_____

_____

_____

_____

_____

_____

_____

_____

_____

PRINCIPLE

Blessed are the merciful.

PRODUCT

They shall obtain mercy.

PRACTICE

_____

_____

_____

PRESCRIPTION

_____

_____

_____

PERSONAL APPLICATION

_____

_____

_____

PRINCIPLE

Blessed are the pure in heart.

PRODUCT

They shall see God.

PRACTICE

_____

_____

_____

PRESCRIPTION

_____

_____

_____

PERSONAL APPLICATION

_____

_____

_____

PRINCIPLE

Blessed are the peacemakers.

PRODUCT

They shall be called sons of God.

PRACTICE

_____

_____

_____

PRESCRIPTION

_____

_____

_____

PERSONAL APPLICATION

_____

_____

_____

PRINCIPLE

Blessed are those who are persecuted for righteousness' sake.

PRODUCT

Theirs is the kingdom of heaven.

PRACTICE

_____

_____

_____

PRESCRIPTION

_____

_____

_____

PERSONAL APPLICATION

_____

_____

_____

QUESTFILE 12.2

Salt and Light   Discuss with your parents the similitudes of salt and light taught by Jesus in Matthew 5:13-16.

Name at least five natural characteristics or uses for each of these.	
SALT	LIGHT

Based on these traits, in what ways are Christians to be like each item?

SALT	LIGHT

What is a specific way your family plans to be salt or light in the next week?

_____
Parent's Signature

PRACTICING PRAYER

QuestTruth

Believers are commanded to pray without ceasing, with thanksgiving, and in accordance with God's Will. The Lord's Prayer thus serves as a pattern for entering God's presence and seeking help for our needs.

 IM4Him: Wow! What a night! I wasn't too sure about a weekend series called "Practicing Prayer," but I'm glad I went. I learned a lot!

 PHETI: Yeah, and the food was great too! Anyway, it hit me—I need to think more about why I pray. So, which category represented the type of praying you do? Is it just the expected thing to do or only for when you're experiencing a crisis?

 IM4Him: Some of my prayers fit in both categories. Honestly, though, most of my prayers are from habit. I always pray before a meal, and I try to always pray for the health and safety of my family. Pastor Scott was right. Prayer is routine for most people, just like taking a shower or brushing your teeth. I've certainly never experienced anything like the story Pastor Scott told.

 PHETI: I haven't either! The people on that plane had to be terrified! Everything was going fine and then, just as they got to the airport, the landing gear wouldn't engage.

 IM4Him: Try to imagine their thoughts when the pilot had to abort the landing and circle above the airport. They had to use up fuel so the plane could make a belly landing.

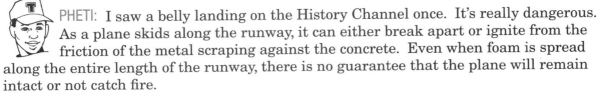 **PHETI:** I saw a belly landing on the History Channel once. It's really dangerous. As a plane skids along the runway, it can either break apart or ignite from the friction of the metal scraping against the concrete. Even when foam is spread along the entire length of the runway, there is no guarantee that the plane will remain intact or not catch fire.

 IM4Him: That's what I call a CRISIS! It's no wonder that, after explaining what to do, the pilot said, "If you believe in God, now is the time to pray!" Like Pastor Scott said, prayer is often the last resort.

PHETI: When people become upset with God and think our prayers aren't answered, it's because we really don't understand what prayer is all about. I remember learning that the Lord's Prayer (Matthew 6:9-13) is a model for our prayers. Pastor Scott really helped me understand what that meant.

IM4Him: Me too. But do you understand the Lord's Prayer well enough to complete the assignment he gave us? We are supposed to explain it to someone else.

PHETI: Well, I think I can use the six characteristics of the Lord's Prayer just as Pastor Scott did. Here are my notes.

FILE SHARING

1. *Worship of God:* "Our Father in heaven, Hallowed be Your name" (6:9). The prayer begins by acknowledging God as the ruler of heaven and earth. When we pray, we must realize that we are entering the presence of the God of all creation.

2. *Commitment to His Will:* "Your kingdom come, Your will be done on earth as it is in heaven" (6:10). To pray effectively, we must be lined up with what God wants. Then God can bless and work through us.

3. *Our needs:* "Give us this day our daily bread" (6:11). Since bread was a common food item eaten with every meal, Jesus used it as a symbol for the everyday needs of life. We are to come to God and ask Him to provide for our daily needs, both physically and spiritually.

4. *Our forgiveness:* "And forgive us our debts, as we forgive our debtors" (6:12). Because we have sinned, we are in debt to Him. Not only must we daily seek His forgiveness, but also be willing to forgive those who have wronged us. Therefore, we ask God to help us develop and maintain our relationships with others as we seek forgiveness and restoration.

5. *Our leadership and protection:* "And do not lead us into temptation, but deliver us from the evil one" (6:13a). We must never forget that Satan is the prince of this world. He seeks to destroy and turn us away from God. We need protection and wisdom for our path into the future.

6. *Worship of God:* "For Yours is the kingdom and the power and the glory forever. Amen" (6:13b). Just as the prayer begins with honoring God, it ends the same way. God must always remain the focus of our prayers because He is the only one who can meet our needs, grant forgiveness and provide direction.

IM4Him: Sounds great! But, like Pastor Scott said, Jesus did more than provide a model for how to pray. He also outlined some important prayer principles to guide us.

 PHETI: Okay, it's your turn. How would you explain the three prayer principles? Let's see your notes.

 IM4Him: Well, the first principle is also in Matthew 6. Here's what I wrote.

 PHETI: Actually, Jesus isn't suggesting that we can't pray in public. He just emphasizes that prayer is a personal conversation between us and God.

> **FILE SHARING**
>
> **Prayer Principle 1:** Prayer should be private and sincere (Matthew 6:5-7). Jesus warned His followers not to be like the hypocrites. When they prayed, they went to the street corner or to the synagogue to stand and pray aloud—loud, long, and wordy. Of course, they were trying to impress others with their spirituality. Jesus condemned those who used prayer to make themselves look holy.

 IM4Him: Right! Prayer is communication with God. It's our opportunity to acknowledge Him as our God, present to Him our needs, seek forgiveness for our sins, ask for future direction and pray for others.

 PHETI: In this passage Jesus also warns against "vain repetitions." The hypocrites that Jesus spoke about not only prayed in public, but they would repeat certain phrases, prayer formulas or teachings of the rabbis. Jesus challenged their thoughtless use of words by providing the model of the Lord's Prayer. That brings us to . . .

 IM4Him: Oh, yes, here it is.

> **FILE SHARING**
>
> **Prayer Principle 2:** Prayer is about humility, not misplaced confidence (Luke 18:9-14). Jesus contrasted the prayers of a Pharisee and a tax collector. Both men went to the Temple to pray; however, their attitudes were quite different. The Pharisee began his prayer by saying, "God, I thank You that I am not like other men." Then he listed how righteous he was. He reminded God that he did not forcibly take things from others; he wasn't unjust, and he didn't commit adultery. He fasted twice each week and gave a tithe of all that he owned. He even thanked God that he wasn't like the tax collector.

PHETI: What a self-righteous hypocrite! But I've heard a few people pray the same way, like they were trying to impress everyone—way different from the tax collector's prayer.

 IM4Him: You're right! Luke 18:13 describes a very different scene. Here are my notes.

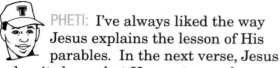 PHETI: I've always liked the way Jesus explains the lesson of His parables. In the next verse, Jesus makes it clear what He wants people to learn—"I tell you, the man [the tax collector] went down to his house justified rather than the other; for everyone who exalts himself will be humbled, and he who humbles himself will be exalted."

 IM4Him: It's just like Pastor Scott explained. People are always trying to impress God with their good works. Although the Pharisee might have been a very good man, he was still a sinner in need of God's mercy. His self-righteous attitude demonstrated that he did not understand his dependence on the Father.

 PHETI: On the other hand, the tax collector ignored any good work that he might have done and humbly approached God asking for forgiveness. As a result of his humility, Jesus said, the tax collector's prayer was answered.

 IM4Him: Here's the last prayer principle. It's the one that really helped me.

FILE SHARING

Prayer Principle 3: Prayer acknowledges God's divine plan and control (Matthew 11:25-30). This principle is difficult to understand and sometimes hard to accept. But the reason is simple—people believe that when they pray for something, God will automatically grant it. This belief sees prayer as some type of magic wand that will make every wish come true. But that's not what Jesus teaches in this passage.

PHETI: I'll have to admit, until Pastor Scott explained this principle, I had never realized how my prayers relate to the accomplishment of God's plan.

 IM4Him: Me too. But that's why Jesus points out these two very important facts about how God accomplishes His plan.

 PHETI: It's mind-boggling! I can understand why Tim brought up all these questions: Is God really listening? How do our prayers affect His Will? Does He always answer us?

 IM4Him: Pastor Scott's response was good when he said that our feelings can change, but God never changes. He is always trustworthy. Prayer is a time to be honest with God about what we're thinking and what we want. We have to recognize that God is the One who is ultimately in control.

 PHETI: At the same time, we can hinder God's response to our prayers. That's why Pastor Scott said we have to ask ourselves these questions about our own prayer life:

- Am I praying with the wrong motives?
- Have I confessed my sins to God?
- Am I faithfully reading and studying the Bible?

 IM4Him: Sometimes our prayers are not answered because we ask for things that are solely for our own pleasure (James 4:3). Of course, that doesn't mean that God does not want us to enjoy ourselves. But prayer is more than just getting stuff. God is not a supernatural vending machine ready to dispense goodies whenever we ask. Prayer is communication with God about the really important things in life.

FILE SHARING

1. Jesus reminds us that we don't know everything that God is going to do ("hidden these things"). We can't just go and pick up a copy of "God's Plan for Life" at the local bookstore and read what's going to happen. Jesus makes it very clear that there are just some things that we aren't going to know or understand.

2. Jesus clearly teaches that God always does what He knows to be good and right ("for it seemed good in your sight"). Although we may ask God to answer a prayer in a certain way, He may choose to provide a different answer. It's not because He didn't hear us or He doesn't care. It's because He knows all things, from the beginning to the end, and His answer is a part of His divine plan.

PHETI: And, according to Isaiah 59:1-2, unconfessed sin separates us from God. In our prayers we need to confess our sins and ask for forgiveness. The Lord's Prayer is the perfect model.

 IM4Him: I thought it was really interesting what Pastor Scott said about idols. The prophet Ezekiel (14:3) made it very clear that idolatry is a sin and can hinder our prayers. But I never thought about the fact that idols are not always made of wood and stone. Anything that becomes more important than God—popularity, grades, athletic or music ability—can be an idol. If these things become more important than our relationship with God, God may withhold the answer to our prayers.

 PHETI: What he said about idols was interesting. But I never thought about how prayer is connected to reading and studying the Bible. Now I understand what Jesus meant in John 15:7: "If you abide in Me, and My words abide in you, you will ask what you desire, and it shall be done for you."

 IM4Him: It is through Scripture that God reveals Himself to us. If we want to know Him better we need to spend more time in His Word. As Pastor Scott said, the effectiveness of our prayers is directly related to our relationship to God.

 PHETI: So, did you post the "Rules for Prayer" next to your computer like Pastor Scott suggested? Since we all spend so much time on the computer, that's a great idea.

 IM4Him: Actually, I had a better idea. I posted each of the five rules in a different place. My computer area is a mess, so the list would have been lost. I chose places in my room where I would constantly notice each rule. For example:

FACTOID

There are at least 19 recorded instances of Jesus praying while on earth, beginning at His baptism until just before His ascension. In all His recorded prayers, Jesus addressed God as "Father."

Rule 1: Be yourself! is posted on my mirror in the bathroom. I wanted it to be the first rule I see each day—a reminder that I not only need to be myself with God, but with others as well. I need to be honest in all of my relationships, especially with God. Through prayer I can communicate with God my true needs and feelings.

Rule 2: Be disciplined! is posted on my desk. Not only am I reminded to be disciplined about doing my schoolwork, but disciplined in my prayer life as well. I need to consciously set aside time—each day—to pray. It's important to be regular. It's not the amount of time, but the frequency, that's important.

Rule 3: Don't judge prayers by feelings! is posted by my telephone. I put it there because so many times telephone calls become so emotional. I've got to remember that the single goal of prayer is to communicate with God, not to receive an emotional high. When Jesus taught about prayer, He never said anything about feelings.

Rule 4: Allow yourself to be silent! is posted by my bed. I always do a lot of thinking when I go to bed at night. This is a good reminder to be quiet and to think about God. Pastor Scott called it meditation. He said that meditation does not mean that you go into some kind of mysterious trance. Meditation is simply bringing thoughts to your mind that will move your heart toward God.

Rule 5: Don't focus on your prayer's results! is posted on the door to my room because I want it to be the first thing I see when I enter my room and the last thing I see as I leave. I'm just like everybody else. When I ask for something, I want it now! But prayer is not like that. Like Pastor Scott said, prayer is like watching a plant grow. You can do it if you want, but it's not going to be all that satisfying. Plants grow a little every day, but our eyes are unable to see the changes taking place. Prayer is like that. Prayer does change things; but it does so according to God's timetable.

 PHETI: I never thought about posting the rules in different parts of my room. That's really a great idea. Like I said at the beginning, I wouldn't call tonight's meeting a prayer meeting, but it sure got me to thinking about prayer, practicing it more I hope. See ya later!

FACTOID

1. Prayer should be humble. (Psalm 10:17; Luke 18:13-14)
2. Prayer should be bold. (1 John 5:13-15)
3. Prayer should be in faith. (Hebrews 11:6)
4. Prayer should be sincere. (Psalm 145:18
5. Prayer should be simple. (Matthew 6:7)
6. Prayer should be persistent. (Luke 18:7; Colossians 4:2)
7. Prayer should be definite. (Psalm 27:4; Acts 12:5)
8. Prayer should be in accord with God's will. (1 John 5:14)

Jesus Prayed

He prayed as He stood in Jordan
To begin a mission of love (Luke 3:21);
He prayed before the break of morn
For guidance from above (Mark 1:35).
He prayed beyond all night before He called
The twelve to follow Him (Luke 6:12);
He prayed beyond the close of day
In twilight shadows dim (Matthew 14:23).

He prayed for human confidence—
For faith to be made bold (Luke 9:18);
He prayed till Heaven glorified
His person and His goal (Luke 9:29).
He prayed with joy at their return
With hearts inspired and blest (Luke 10:21);
He prayed in tears to raise the dead
And shamed the doubting guest (John 11:41).

He prayed and taught them how to pray
With words to guide the way (Luke 11:1);
He prayed from His own troubled soul
And cried, "What can I say?" (John 12:27).
He prayed twice on His knees,
And then fell on His face (Luke 22:41);
He prayed till sweat became as drops of blood
While drinking sin's disgrace (Luke 22:44).

He prayed for those about Him
Then for all as yet unborn (John 17);
He prayed for one who stood in fear
Beside the fire of scorn (Luke 22:32).
He prayed, "Father, forgive them,
They know not what they do" (Luke 23:34).
He prayed at Calvary's darkest hour,
"O Father, where are You?" (Mark 15:34).
He prayed at last with dying breath,
And bowed His head in peace;
"Into Thy hands I commend my spirit";
And this earthly prayer life ceased (Luke 23:46).

–Adapted from J. Tillman Lake

QuestFile 13.1

Family Chatroom/What's Wrong with This Prayer? Interact with your parents, another adult mentor or your classmates to discuss what's wrong with the following approaches to prayer. Write their suggestions for better handling the situations.

1. *In desperation Rick retreats to his bedroom, falls to his knees by his bed and begins to cry out to the Lord. "Lord, I need help. If something doesn't happen soon, I'm going to fail this semester. Then I won't be able to play baseball in the spring and my dad's gonna kill me. Please help me mark the right answers on the make-up test tomorrow. If you will, I promise to study like I'm supposed to next semester. Give me this last chance, please Lord!"*

   _____

   _____

   _____

   _____

2. *Mr. Harris is a local businessman who has a reputation for less-than-honest deals. However, each year he has been featured at the mayor's prayer breakfast because he prays with such beautiful language, and people are always impressed. However, this year the mayor chose a personal friend to lead the main prayer. Mr. Harris is more than unhappy about being preempted from this annual honor. He has promised to make sure the mayor is defeated in the next election.*

   _____

   _____

   _____

   _____

3. Robbie has been impressed with Mr. Akeem's dedication to prayer. Regardless of how busy things are at the store, several times a day he kneels on a prayer rug facing toward the east. Speaking in a different language, he repeats the following phrases again and again. "O God, O God, O God!—O Lord, O Lord, O Lord!—O living, O immortal, O living, O immortal!—O Creator of the heavens and the earth! . . ." One time at the airport Robbie was surprised to see Mr. Akeem kneel and pray right in front of everyone.

_____

_____

_____

_____

_____

_____

4. When it's Jenny's turn to pray, whether at church or home, she generally prays as follows: "Dear Lord, thank you for all your blessings. Forgive our sins. We pray for all the missionaries and sick people. Help us to live better. In Jesus' name, Amen."

_____

_____

_____

_____

_____

_____

_____

Parent's Signature

142

QuestFile 13.2

Packets on Prayer Summarize what you have learned about prayer.

1. What is prayer?

_____

_____

_____

_____

_____

_____

2. Why are Christians commanded to pray?

_____

_____

_____

_____

_____

_____

_____

3. What are the subjects we should include as modeled in the Lord's Prayer?

_____

_____

_____

_____

_____

4. What negative attitudes or actions are we warned against in practicing prayer?

_____

_____

_____

_____

_____

5. Why is it so important to pray in accordance with God's will (1 John 5:14-15)?

_____

_____

_____

_____

_____

_____

_____

6. How can we be assured God will answer our prayers?

_____

_____

_____

_____

_____

_____

7. In what four ways does God answer our prayers?

_____

_____

_____

_____

_____

_____

8. What positive commands does Scripture provide regarding how we should pray?

_____

_____

_____

_____

_____

_____

_____

TEACHING IN PARABLES

QuestTruth

Jesus taught in parables to illustrate the truths He presented, with the ultimate objective that believers would obey His words, not just hear them.

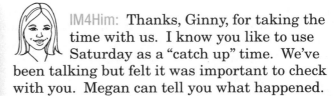

IM4Him: Thanks, Ginny, for taking the time with us. I know you like to use Saturday as a "catch up" time. We've been talking but felt it was important to check with you. Megan can tell you what happened.

QTee: Well, I really got into it last night. It seems like everybody in my family is stressed out. Mom and Dad have a lot of new responsibilities at their jobs, and my brother Jackson is taking extra classes at college so he can graduate early. I'm trying out for our school's first drama production and playing in a golf tournament at the same time. We just didn't expect to be so busy this year.

Anyway, Mom and Dad started reminding me to use my time wisely in the next few weeks. So I told them that if I run out of time, I'll just cut out some non-essentials—like church. I was only kidding, but they became furious.

So then I reacted, "Salvation is not based on works, right? What difference does it make if I don't want to go to church?" Me and my mouth! I wish I had never said that.

I immediately apologized and things are better between us. But I still think my question deserves an answer. What if I don't want to go to church, read my Bible, or pray? What's the big deal if I skip these things for a while until my schedule isn't so stressed?

IM4Him: I think Megan's question is a good one. We both want to know what you think about what happened—and also how to fix it up with her folks.

2B4Givn: Your question, "What if I don't want to?" reminded me of my freshman year in college. I know that college is still in the future for both of you, but I learned a valuable lesson during that first year.

I graduated from high school in the top 5 percent of my class. My SAT and ACT scores were great. I had no trouble getting into the college I chose. My first real shock came when I registered for the fall term. I had to take all of these "101" courses. There was English 101, Biology 101, History 101—well, you get the picture.

2B4Givn: The problem was, I didn't want to waste my time on those basic courses. I wanted to get started on my major and take more advanced courses. I was sure that I was ready for a bigger challenge. Little did I realize how important those basic courses would be to my future success in college, and in life.

 QTee: I'm not quite sure what all of this has to do with my question. You see, I like church and all, especially seeing my friends. But I just don't have time right now.

 2B4Givn: Let me put it this way—now that you're in high school, you've taken another step toward adulthood. In addition to your school classes, you are in one that I call Life 101. Although there are no homework assignments and you won't be getting a grade, there are still many valuable basic lessons that you'll need to learn.

For example, have you ever said to someone, "That's not fair!"? One of the lessons of Life 101 is that life is not always fair. As you get older, you will face many situations that just aren't fair, and there's not a thing you can do about it. It's up to you to accept that fact and go on with life.

Another Life 101 lesson occurs when you get your first job. Often students make excuses for not getting their homework done on time. Let me assure you, your boss would not be impressed if you give an excuse for why your work didn't get done. In fact, you would probably lose your job. Life 101, lesson 2 is: Bosses are a lot less forgiving than teachers.

QTee: I get your point! Still, it's no big deal—I know lots of people who do the "Christian stuff" only when it's convenient.

2B4Givn: Wait! I'm not finished. As a result of your disagreement with your parents, you have stumbled upon another of life's lessons. It's the one that I had to learn in taking basic college courses. It goes like this: For some reason or other, there will always be things in life that we don't want to do. However, if we don't do them, we will ultimately lose the benefit. Actually, this is a lesson that Jesus taught throughout His ministry.

IM4Him: Sounds like the bottom line of a parable—just can't remember which one right now.

 2B4Givn: Exactly! But before I give you an example, remember that a parable is a story with two meanings. One meaning is obvious and relates to life or nature. The other is more obscure; it provides instruction and gives a higher purpose to the story. This process is called transcendence (sorry for the college word). It's a story that has application to more important areas of life.

 IM4Him: In simpler terms, a parable is an earthly story with a heavenly meaning. Jesus taught in parables a lot. Sometimes people understood and sometimes they didn't. Seems like Jesus purposely wanted His hearers to be puzzled. Why did He do that?

 2B4Givn: First of all, by teaching in parables Jesus was fulfilling Old Testament prophecy—"I will open My mouth in parables, I will utter things kept secret from the foundation of the world" (Matthew 13:35). This prophecy was first spoken in Psalm 78:2. Jesus spoke to people who planted and sowed, fished, constructed buildings or took care of sheep. He spoke in terms that His listeners would understand. This also makes His teachings much clearer to us today.

Although Jesus used parables to teach various lessons, a major theme was to show what it truly means to follow Him. Many who called themselves followers of Jesus were unwilling to pay the price of true discipleship. By using parables, Jesus was able to illustrate that they didn't actually practice what they said they said they believed. He would then explain why it is important to act consistently with what you believe. In other words, Jesus challenged His followers to "walk the talk," not just "talk the talk."

 IM4Him: I've heard that phrase "walk the talk" before. I never thought about it being a principle that Jesus taught.

 2B4Givn: Hold on! I didn't mean to say that "walk the talk" are words found in the Bible. But it is a biblical principle that Jesus clearly taught. For centuries, the rabbis and Pharisees used spiritual sounding words but continued sinful, corrupt practices. Jesus wanted His followers to live consistently with what they professed to believe—in other words, walk the talk. Through parables Jesus was able to emphasize this important principle.

QTee: Can you maybe get to the point? Do you think the parables hold the answer to my question, "What if I don't want to"?

 2B4Givn: I'll let you be the judge of that. Two of the clearest examples of walking the talk are found in Matthew 7 (the parable of the two builders) and Luke 6 (the parable of the blind leading the blind). Although the parable of the two builders is recorded in Matthew 7:24-27, I want you to begin by reading verse 13. Do you see anything unusual about the way these verses are organized? I'll wait.

PROCESSING

 IM4Him: Everything is presented in "twos." In verses 13-14 there are two gates, two ways, two destinations, and two groups of people. In verses 17-20 there are two kinds of trees and two kinds of fruit. There are two groups at the judgment described in verses 21-23. In verses 24-27 there are two kinds of builders, building on two different foundations.

 2B4Givn: Do you see what Jesus was doing? He was trying to show His listeners that there are only two ways of doing things—the world's way or God's way. There is the wide gate that "leads to destruction" or the narrow gate that "leads to life" (7:13-14).

For a minute, let's take a closer look at the parable of the two builders. Sarah, I'm sure you remember the story that Dad told us about his first summer job.

 QTee: I don't know what you're talking about. What's the story? And what's the connection?

 2B4Givn: Let me tell the story, and I think the connection will be obvious. Dad said that if you travel north of Toledo, Ohio, on I-75, you will enter Monroe, Michigan, shortly after crossing the Michigan state line. Although you can't see the city of Monroe from the Interstate, you can't miss the two smokestacks to the east. Each stack is over 500 feet tall. They are part of one of the largest electric power production facilities in the United States. He told us that if we ever travel on that stretch of highway, we should take a look at the north stack to make sure it is still standing. Here's why.

As a college student, he spent a summer working at that job site. He was part of a 15-member crew assigned to prepare the base pads that would become the sub-foundation for that stack. Each pad was about 10 feet square. Before the concrete could be poured, it was his crew's job to make sure that the sand and gravel were tightly compacted.

Although it was not a hard job physically, the heat and humidity in mid-July made the task very difficult. The base pads were at the bottom of an excavated pit nearly 25 feet deep. The air was stale, hot and humid! Dad said that all they could think about was preparing those pads as quickly as possible and then climbing back to the surface. But the foreman wasn't cooperative. Standing at the top of the pit, he would keep signaling that the pads needed more pounding.

Dad said the foreman's frustration must have become obvious, because he climbed down the 25-foot series of ladders to where Dad was working. Dad knew that he was in trouble, but the foreman didn't say anything at first. He just stepped into the area where Dad had been compacting. His foot sank about three inches into the wet sand. He then turned to Dad and simply said, "If the foundation ain't right, the building's gonna fall."

Nothing else was said. He just walked away to inspect the other pad areas. But Dad said that he has never forgotten the embarrassment of that moment. Every time he remembers the north stack standing over 500 feet high, he thinks about the foreman's words, "If the foundation ain't right, the building's gonna fall." I think of Dad's story every time I read the parable of the two builders—a story so familiar that we can miss its importance if we're not careful.

IM4Him: I think I understand the connection. Tell me if I've got it right. Jesus described two builders—one built his house on the rock and the other on sand. When the rains came, the flood rose and the wind blew. The house built upon the rock stood firm. However, the house built upon the sand collapsed. The story was simple and easy for Jesus' listeners to understand. But, like all parables, the story has a second meaning.

The house represents a person's life. The rain, flood, and wind represent the trials and difficulties that we are sure to experience. The meaning of the two foundations is very important. Jesus stated the truth of this story in verse 26: "But everyone who hears these sayings of Mine, and does not do them, will be like a foolish man who built his house on the sand." Megan, what do you think the rock foundation represented?

QTee: Based on verse 24, I would have to say "obedience." Jesus said, "Therefore, whoever hears these sayings of mine, and does them, I will liken him to the wise man who built his house on the rock."

 2B4Givn: You're exactly right. Those who build upon what God teaches will be able to withstand the problems they face in life. Those who ignore His teachings and follow this world will not. Jesus reminded His listeners that there must be consistency between belief and action. To pretend one thing and do something else is foolish.

Let me remind you of something I said earlier. The reason Jesus emphasized the two kinds of builders and foundations was because of the inconsistent way that many of Israel's spiritual leaders lived. Their hypocrisy was evident to everyone. They were in positions of spiritual leadership, yet they interpreted what God said according to what they wanted to believe. With the simplest possible illustration, Jesus pointed out that they were building on a foundation of sand.

Building on the Sand
Hears but does nothing

Building on the Rock
1. Comes to Me
2. Hears My sayings
3. Does them

 QTee: So we must maintain consistency between what we believe and what we actually do. That makes sense, but it's sure easier said than done.

FACTOID

A parable can range from a short, compact saying to a complete story. By using illustrations from daily life, Jesus identified with the people and made His point in language they could easily understand.

 2B4Givn: Perhaps this was one of the reasons your parents were so upset with you. They are concerned that you continue to "walk the talk." They know that doing otherwise can lead to destruction.

 QTee: You're probably right. I wasn't trying to be rebellious or anything. But I'm beginning to see how important it is to be consistent.

2B4Givn: I think that there is another parable your parents wanted you to learn. In Luke 6:40, Jesus said, "A disciple is not above his teacher, but everyone who is perfectly trained will be like his teacher."

Jesus pointed out how important the influence of one life is on another. In order to become spiritually mature, we should follow a person who provides a strong spiritual example. Christianity is a way of life that is learned from Christian models. Removing ourselves from godly teaching and influence can hurt our growth in the Lord.

 QTee: Now I get it! My parents were trying to show me that I need to consistently live out my faith. They also want me to copy my life after them and other godly people at church. What I said to them—and how I said it—was wrong.

 2B4Givn: Congratulations! You've just passed your first test in Life 101. You get *A+* for the effort.

Parables from the Sermon on the Mount
Take notes as the class members report on their assigned parable.

**Reference: Matthew 7:1-5
Luke 6:41-42**

Speck vs. Plank

Application: _____

_____

_____

_____

_____

_____

_____

_____

Reference: Luke 6:39-40

Blind Guides

Application: _____

_____

_____

_____

_____

_____

_____

_____

Reference: Matthew 7:15-20
Luke 6:43-45

Good Trees and Good Fruit

Application: _____
_____
_____
_____
_____
_____
_____

Reference: Matthew 7:13-14

Two Gates and Two Ways

Application: _____
_____
_____
_____
_____
_____
_____

Reference: Matthew 7:24-27
Luke 6:46-49

Two Builders

Application: _____
_____
_____
_____
_____
_____
_____

Family Chatroom/Listening and Doing

Jesus taught that the solid foundation of life is based on doing as He said, not just hearing His words. Discuss with your parents and list some of their answers.

1. Why do most Christians find it harder to obey Jesus' teaching, rather than just hearing it? _____

_____

_____

_____

2. Why is it important for Christians to "walk the talk"—actually <u>do</u> what Jesus taught (what they say they believe)? _____

_____

_____

_____

3. How can doing what you don't want to do make you a better person?

_____

_____

_____

4. What suggestions do you have for teens who want to obey (not just talk about) Jesus' teachings? _____

_____

_____

_____

_____
Parent's Signature

STUDY HIS LIFE   FIND DIRECTION   KNOW HIM   HAVE A RIGHT ATTITUDE
BECOME CHRIST-LIKE   KNOW GOD'S WORD   SEARCH FOR ANSWERS
MAKE MATURE CHOICES   COMMIT MYSELF   HAVE GOOD RELATIONSHIPS
STUDY HIS LIFE   FIND DIRECTION   KNOW HIM   HAVE A RIGHT ATTITUDE
BECOME CHRIST-LIKE   KNOW GOD'S WORD   SEARCH FOR ANSWERS
MAKE MATURE CHOICES   COMMIT MYSELF   HAVE GOOD RELATIONSHIPS
STUDY HIS LIFE   FIND DIRECTION   KNOW HIM   HAVE A RIGHT ATTITUDE
BECOME CHRIST-LIKE   KNOW GOD'S WORD   SEARCH FOR ANSWERS
MAKE MATURE CHOICES   COMMIT MYSELF   HAVE GOOD RELATIONSHIPS
STUDY HIS LIFE   FIND DIRECTION   KNOW HIM   HAVE A RIGHT ATTITUDE
BECOME CHRIST-LIKE   KNOW GOD'S WORD   SEARCH FOR ANSWERS
MAKE MATURE CHOICES   COMMIT MYSELF   HAVE GOOD RELATIONSHIPS
STUDY HIS LIFE   FIND DIRECTION   KNOW HIM   HAVE A RIGHT ATTITUDE
BECOME CHRIST-LIKE   KNOW GOD'S WORD   SEARCH FOR ANSWERS
MAKE MATURE CHOICES   COMMIT MYSELF   HAVE GOOD RELATIONSHIPS
STUDY HIS LIFE   FIND DIRECTION   KNOW HIM   HAVE A RIGHT ATTITUDE
BECOME CHRIST-LIKE   KNOW GOD'S WORD   SEARCH FOR ANSWERS
MAKE MATURE CHOICES   COMMIT MYSELF   HAVE GOOD RELATIONSHIPS
STUDY HIS LIFE   FIND DIRECTION   KNOW HIM   HAVE A RIGHT ATTITUDE
BECOME CHRIST-LIKE   KNOW GOD'S WORD   SEARCH FOR ANSWERS
MAKE MATURE CHOICES   COMMIT MYSELF   HAVE GOOD RELATIONSHIPS
STUDY HIS LIFE   FIND DIRECTION   KNOW HIM   HAVE A RIGHT ATTITUDE
BECOME CHRIST-LIKE   KNOW GOD'S WORD   SEARCH FOR ANSWERS
MAKE MATURE CHOICES   COMMIT MYSELF   HAVE GOOD RELATIONSHIPS
STUDY HIS LIFE   FIND DIRECTION   KNOW HIM   HAVE A RIGHT ATTITUDE
BECOME CHRIST-LIKE   KNOW GOD'S WORD   SEARCH FOR ANSWERS
MAKE MATURE CHOICES   COMMIT MYSELF   HAVE GOOD RELATIONSHIPS

Walk the Talk!

THE POWER OF FAITH

QUESTTRUTH

Faith is firm belief that results in action. Without it, we can't please God. With it, we receive justification, righteousness, grace for living and eternal salvation.

 Gr8-1: Thanks for the call this afternoon. I'm sorry I wasn't home, but things are a little hectic right now.

 UthPstr: Don't worry about it. I heard that your grandfather is very ill and that you and your family are heading to Georgia to see him. I'll be praying for his recovery. Is there anything else I can do to help?

 Gr8-1: Thanks, I appreciate you just praying right now. Grandpa means a lot to my dad, and to me too. He's quite a man of faith, and he and my dad have always been very close. Dad has told me so many stories about him. They always make me wonder, *How can I ever have as much faith as my grandfather has?*

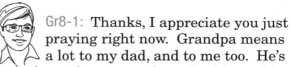 **UthPstr:** Your dad has told me a lot about your grandfather too. He has had some amazing experiences. It reminds me of a biography I'm reading—the story of Eliza George. At the age of 94, Mrs. George was tramping the trails of tribal Africa, taking the gospel to people in the land from where her ancestors had been removed as slaves. Here's a clip from the introduction.

FILE SHARING

Born in America of parents who were former slaves, Eliza was the third of 11 children. After high school, she attended and graduated from Central Texas College in Waco, Texas. As a result of her academic record and strong Christian character, she was asked to join the faculty of the school.

One morning during a chapel service, Eliza felt God's call to reach her people in Africa. Although it was a surprise to her friends and the faculty at the college, she announced that she was going to Africa as a missionary. She arrived in Monrovia, Liberia, on her 35th birthday.

Over the next 60 years, she shared the gospel throughout the country of Liberia. She established the Bible Industrial Academy where she taught agriculture and tailoring in addition to Bible classes. She built and operated an orphanage that housed and educated 50 children at a time.

She founded the Native Interior Mission where she trained young men and women to work among their own people. She even received the medal of "Grand Commander for the Redemption of Africa."

As her life came to a close, she often talked about that day in chapel when she received the urging from God to go to Africa. She remembered resisting God's call because she feared the hardships she would face. She once confessed that she didn't have sufficient faith to go to another continent, learn a new language and do what had to be done. But she also knew she had to obey God, and she was willing to take the first step. She soon realized that her faith was growing as she trusted God to meet her needs and to use her to accomplish things she never thought possible.

 UthPstr: The lesson that Eliza George learned is the starting point for the answer to your concern about having more faith. Faith increases when we obey God and watch Him work.

 Gr8-1: That's quite a story. I can't believe someone would just go to Africa, not knowing anyone there and not knowing exactly what needed to be done.

 UthPstr: Now you're beginning to see what is meant by "faith." Let me ask you a simple question. Why did Jesus perform miracles?

 Gr8-1: I suppose it was because He cared about people and tried to help them, like healing them or giving them food to eat.

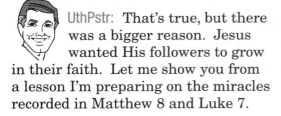 **UthPstr:** That's true, but there was a bigger reason. Jesus wanted His followers to grow in their faith. Let me show you from a lesson I'm preparing on the miracles recorded in Matthew 8 and Luke 7.

When Jesus entered the city of Capernaum, He was asked to go to a Roman officer's house to heal his servant. Luke picks up the story first with a delegation of Jewish elders presenting the centurion's request. They begged him earnestly, saying that the one for whom He should do this was worthy, "for he loves our nation, and has built us a synagogue." (By the way, the archaeological ruins of this synagogue

FILE SHARING

are open to visitors today.) The centurion was a man of influence and power. As a Roman captain of a 100-man army brigade (cent = 100), it was most unusual for him to have such respect among the Jews.

In response, Jesus headed to the centurion's home. However, the centurion approached Him on the way and said, "Lord, I am not worthy that You should come under my roof" (Matthew 8:8). Jewish tradition declared that a Jew who entered a Gentile's house was ceremonially defiled. The centurion, undoubtedly familiar with this law, perhaps felt unworthy of having Jesus suffer such an inconvenience for his sake.

He made a remarkable statement to Jesus—"For I also am a man under authority, having soldiers under me. And I say to this one, 'Go,' and he goes; and to another, 'come,' and he comes; and to my servant, 'do this,' and he does it." The centurion's point was this: As a soldier, his authority over others resulted from his position. The chain of command gave him power to command those of less authority. When he spoke, he represented all the power of Rome's mighty empire, whose authority stood behind him.

In his statement, the centurion acknowledged that Jesus also operated under authority—the authority of God. When Jesus spoke, all the power of God Himself spoke through Him. The Roman soldier knew that Jesus did not need to come into his house. He expressed full confidence in Jesus, knowing He could heal from a distance by merely speaking a word. All power in heaven and on earth had been committed to Him. Jesus had authority over nature, disease, and death. The centurion acknowledged what the Jewish leaders denied.

The Bible states, "Then Jesus said to the centurion, 'Go your way; and as you have believed, so let it be done for you.' And his servant was healed that same hour." Jesus commented about the centurion, "I have not found such great faith, not even in Israel!"

Gr8-1: The centurion acted on his faith. It seems like he just trusted Jesus to be the solution to his problem.

UthPstr: You're right! Hebrews 11:6 states it this way: "But without faith it is impossible to please Him, for he who comes to God must believe that He is, and that He is a rewarder of those who diligently seek Him." It is one thing to say that you have faith. It's quite a different thing to act upon that faith.

UthPstr: The disciples learned valuable lessons about authority and faith from this Roman centurion. And Jesus clearly demonstrated to them that He had God-given power. After all, a miracle is something only God can do.

Gr8-1: I remember your saying that before. But right now I'm thinking mostly about my grandpa. We know he's ready to meet the Lord, but we are going to miss him terribly. I'm not sure which passage of Scripture you're referring to, but I'm sure it has to do with raising someone from the dead.

UthPstr: I understand your feelings. Still, I know your grandfather is looking forward to the resurrection. The passage I'm referring to is a great story in Luke. Entering the city of Nain, Jesus was followed by His disciples along with a large crowd. Nearing the gate of the city, He saw a dead man being carried out. Death is always a time for grief and sadness. But this death was particularly difficult because the man was the only son of a widow. This woman, who had already lost her husband, had now lost her only son. It's no wonder that she was weeping uncontrollably.

Look at what Luke said: "When the Lord saw her, He had compassion on her and said to her, 'Do not weep.' Then He came and touched the open coffin, and those who carried him stood still. And He said, 'Young man, I say to you, arise.' So he who was dead sat up and began to speak. And He presented him to his mother" (Luke 7:13-15).

Jesus began by expressing words of comfort. Then He touched the open coffin. This act got the attention of the onlookers because, according to Jewish teaching, touching an open coffin was an act of defilement. But Jesus was not concerned about being called unclean. He then said "Arise" to the dead man. To the amazement of everyone, the young man sat up and began speaking to his mother.

Look at what Luke said next: "Then the fear came upon all, and they glorified God, saying, 'A great prophet has risen up among us'; and, 'God has visited His people'" (Luke 7:16). Jesus had done many miracles before, but raising someone from the dead was an ultimate display of power.

Gr8-1: I understand how personally seeing the miracles helped prove that Jesus was really God. It increased the faith of the people who saw them each time one was performed.

UthPstr: If you stop and think about it, the centurion demonstrated more faith than one of Jesus' disciples. After Jesus' resurrection, "doubting Thomas" wanted to see the nail prints in Jesus' hands and feet before he would believe. Jesus granted his request but then said, "Thomas, because you have seen Me, you have believed. Blessed are those who have not seen and yet have believed" (John 20:29).

I think that last phrase really describes your granddad. Tim, let me show you—in a practical way—how you can have the same faith as him. There are two very important principles that you need to remember. Your friends tell me that you like the water. Is that true?

FACTOID

The centurion was a military officer who commanded 100 men. Our army today, like the Roman army of Jesus' day, has a chain of command. Commissioned officers begin with a lieutenant who commands a platoon. Platoons make up a company that is typically under the command of a captain. Several companies make up a battalion, and a number of battalions make up a division. The Lord responded to the centurion in military terms because that was the life he understood.

 Gr8-1: Sure, I love to swim and water ski—go every time I can.

 UthPstr: That's good. If you haven't been to Niagara Falls, I'm sure you've heard about it. A few years ago a couple, as their first date, decided to go over the falls in a specially built barrel that cost almost $25,000. Fortunately, they survived their trip. In a later interview, they were asked to describe the scariest part of the trip.

"It was the 15 seconds," the man said, "from the time our barrel hit the river until we went over the falls. For 15 seconds everything was in the hands of the river."

 Gr8-1: Weird story! I can guarantee you that I would never go over Niagara Falls in a barrel. I'm not that much of a thrill-seeker.

 UthPstr: I'm sure you wouldn't. But that story illustrates the first principle. If you want to have more faith, YOU NEED TO BE INTENTIONAL ABOUT DOING THE WILL OF GOD RIGHT FROM THE START!

UthPstr: The dictionary defines "intentional" as "doing something on purpose." Consider what this couple did. They made an intentional decision to go over the falls in a barrel. They spent a large sum of money to build a barrel that would keep them safe. They made the journey down to the edge of the river. They got into the barrel and allowed the barrel to be pushed into the river. Once they made their initial decision, they didn't let anything stop them from achieving their goal.

 Gr8-1: I guess it's one thing to jump into any old barrel versus preparing one you can depend on.

 UthPstr: Right! The first step to having more faith is determining to follow the will of God for your life, no matter what! At times, you're going to feel like the couple did during that 15 seconds. You won't have any control over what's going on around you. But instead of your life being in the hands of the river, your life will be in the hands of God.

 Gr8-1: I remember a great verse in John that you taught us—7:17, I think—about how we will know what God wants only after we are willing to obey.

 UthPstr: That fits perfectly. After you are willing to be intentional about doing the will of God, you will be ready for the second principle. But before I share that principle with you, I want you to read some verses and tell me what Satan offered Jesus during His time of temptation. Turn to Matthew 4:1-11.

Gr8-1: It looks like Satan offered Jesus power, fame, and wealth. Satan said he would give Jesus everything the world could provide.

UthPstr: I'm not asking you to answer this question, but what would it be like if you had all the power, fame, and wealth this world offers? It would be really tempting, wouldn't it? That brings us to our second principle.

UthPstr: One of the most difficult things for a person to do is surrender control of his or her own life. We all like to be in charge—to make our own decisions. However, if you want to have more faith, YOU MUST SURRENDER TO GOD ON A DAY-BY-DAY BASIS. Surrendering to the Lord means giving up your own agenda and letting God work out His plan through you.

You see, it's not enough to jump into the flow of God's river. You need to stay in the flow as well.

 Gr8-1: What if the couple's barrel had hit the boulders along the shore, or if the barrel had been grabbed from the water just seconds from the edge of the falls? Obviously, all of their intentions and preparations would have meant nothing.

 UthPstr: When it comes to faith, so many Christians are like the couple in the barrel. They have really good intentions. They want to trust God. They want to have more faith. At times, they are even willing to take risks and jump into the flow of God's river. But all too often, when things get difficult and scary, they want to give up. Faith comes as we stay in the river, securely in God's hand, and allow Him to work through us.

Gr8-1: Thanks for taking the time to talk with me. I hope you'll pray that God will help me with becoming intentional about my faith and learning to surrender to Him daily. I really feel a lot better now.

UthPstr: Trust me, I will pray for you! I'll also be praying for your family during these difficult days. Have a safe trip!

> **FACTOID**
>
> Faith is just believing
>   What God says He will do.
> He will never fail us,
>   His promises are true.
> If we but receive Him,
>   His children we become.
> Faith is just believing
>   What God says He will do.

Family Chatroom/Faith Walk
Interact with your parents or other mentor and record their responses.

1. Who, in our family, is a good example of strong faith? On what basis?

_____

_____

_____

_____

_____

2. What things have helped your faith grow throughout your life?

_____

_____

_____

_____

3. How can teens develop stronger faith?

_____

_____

_____

_____

_____
Parent's Signature

QUESTFILE 15.1

Steps of Faith Facts Record summaries of these Scriptures during class discussion.

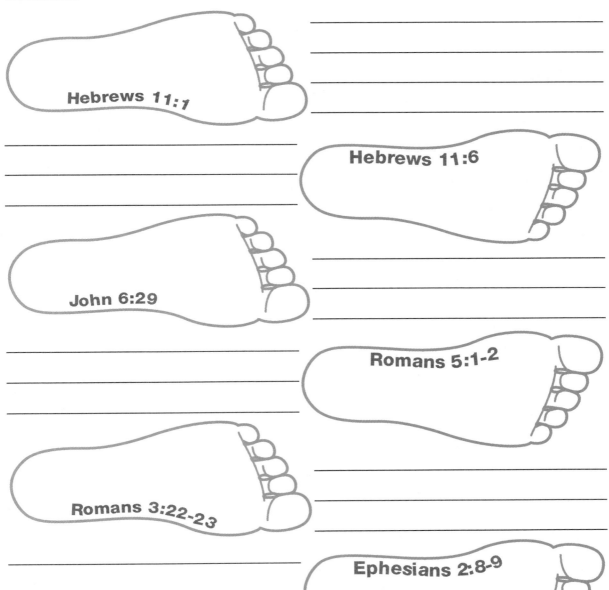

Hebrews 11:1

Hebrews 11:6

John 6:29

Romans 5:1-2

Romans 3:22-23

Ephesians 2:8-9

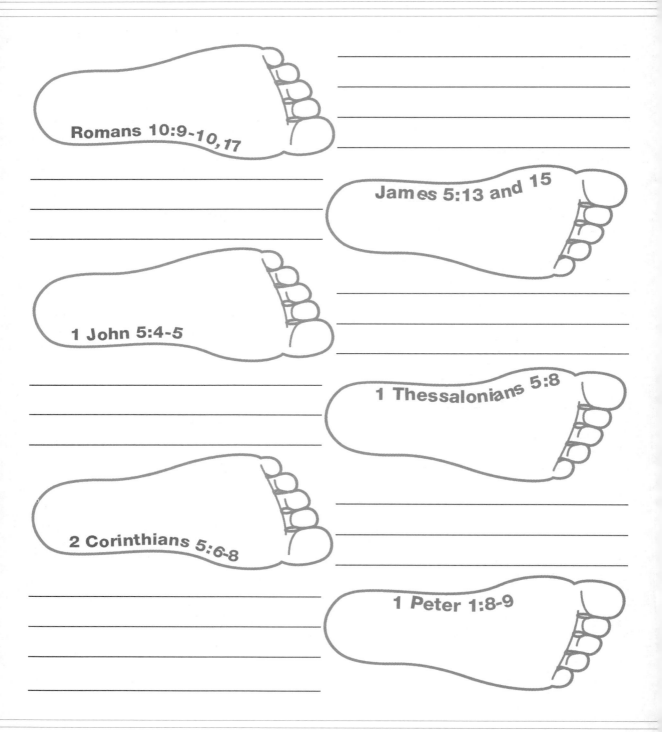

Romans 10:9-10,17

James 5:13 and 15

1 John 5:4-5

1 Thessalonians 5:8

2 Corinthians 5:6-8

1 Peter 1:8-9

THE KINGDOM OF GOD

QuestTruth

The Kingdom of God is sown in the hearts of people through the Word of God. This Word must be received in faith, then in turn produces spiritual fruit in believers.

PHETI: Sorry I'm late for our project meeting. My dad asked me last night to go with him to the men's Bible study this morning. He goes every Friday. He thought today's topic might interest me.

Gr8-1: No problem. There wasn't a lot of new information—just making sure everyone is on task. How was the Bible study? What was the topic?

PHETI: Pastor Ryan's title was "Too much to do—too little time!" It was all about time management. I've been telling my dad lately that I just don't have enough time for everything. I have homework, practice, and chores to do every day. I also help my little brother with his homework almost every night, and there's at least one activity at church that I want to attend during the week.

Gr8-1: Yeah, I know what you mean. No matter how organized I try to be, I can't get everything done. Sometimes I feel like a juggler spinning plates on top of long sticks.

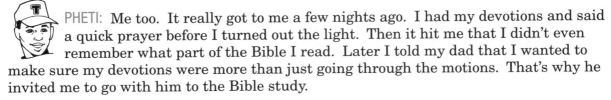

PHETI: Me too. It really got to me a few nights ago. I had my devotions and said a quick prayer before I turned out the light. Then it hit me that I didn't even remember what part of the Bible I read. Later I told my dad that I wanted to make sure my devotions were more than just going through the motions. That's why he invited me to go with him to the Bible study.

Gr8-1: So, did you learn anything interesting? I could use whatever helpful hints you picked up.

PHETI: I think so. For example, Jesus talked about this very problem. Pastor Ryan said that during Jesus' day, people had difficulty seeing the relationship between how they lived daily and their spiritual beliefs. So Jesus provided illustrations—called parables of the Kingdom—to help His hearers understand.

Gr8-1: I know some of the parables, but I didn't know that there was a whole group especially called the parables of the Kingdom. What does that mean?

 PHETI: Pastor Ryan told us that although the word "kingdom" appears in a variety of ways in the Bible, it is used in a very general way with these parables. Kingdom refers to Jesus' work in the heart of His followers—those who will ultimately be in heaven with Him. Eight of these parables are described in Matthew 13 and the ninth one is in Mark 4. I wrote down the description for each parable. Wait while I click in my notes.

FILE SHARING

1. **The Parable of the Sower** (Matthew 13:1-23). In this parable Jesus discusses how the message of the Kingdom is received by various people.

2. **The Parable of the Wheat and the Tares** (13:24-30). Jesus warns that people who pretend to be part of the Kingdom may be able to fool others, but they can't fool God.

3. **The Parable of the Good Seed** (Mark 4:26-29). Jesus teaches that the Kingdom is God's work and it will grow according to His plan.

4. **The Parable of the Mustard Seed** (Matthew 13:31-32). Jesus promises that His Kingdom, although small at the time, would one day become a powerful force in the world.

5. **The Parable of the Leaven** (13:33). Jesus describes the influence of the Kingdom: it quietly, but effectively, spreads among people as it accomplishes its objectives.

6. **The Parable of the Hidden Treasure** (13:44). Jesus places a value upon the Kingdom. He describes it as the most important thing anyone can possess.

7. **The Parable of the Pearl of Great Price** (13:45-46). Jesus continues to describe the value of the Kingdom. This time He says that its value is worth sacrificing everything in order to possess it.

8. **The Parable of the Dragnet** (13:47-50). Jesus warns that a day of judgment is coming when those who are part of the Kingdom will be separated from those who reject it.

9. **The Parable of the Householder** (13:51-52). Jesus tells those who understand the Kingdom that they have a responsibility to share their knowledge with others.

Gr8-1: Wow! That's a lot of information—no wonder you were late. I've heard of most of those parables. What else did Pastor Ryan say?

PHETI: Like I told you, I was concerned about the way that I was treating my Bible study and prayer time. Pastor Ryan's explanation of the parable of the sower really helped me.

He reminded us that Jesus' hearers knew what He meant when He said, "Behold a sower went out to sow." A sower walked along the fields with a sack or basket filled with seeds. He then took a handful of the seeds and spread them over a wide area.

Gr8-1: Yeah, I guess those living in Jesus' day did not have the necessary equipment to plant a large quantity of seeds. Sowing on top of the ground was the easiest way to get the job done.

PHETI: The seed represents God's Word and the sower represents the one who is spreading God's Word. For many years Christians have interpreted the sower as a pastor, preacher, or evangelist. While it's true that these people spread God's Word, the image of the sower is not limited just to them. In this parable, Jesus describes the sower as anyone who shares the message of God's Word. Here are my notes.

FILE SHARING

The seed lands on four different types of soil: the wayside (verse 4), stony places (verse 5), among thorns (verse 7), and on good ground (verse 8). The different types of soil represent the different responses to God's Word.

Wayside—*Wayside is another name for a pathway. On a pathway, the grass is beaten down and the soil is very hard. It's like the paths bordering the fields were made hard by foot traffic and the baking sun. Jesus was saying that some people listen to God's Word with a heart like the hardened path. They seem to be unconcerned with what the gospel says. Truth seems to have no more effect on their heart than water on a stone.*

Stony Places—*This type of soil is illustrated by the pioneers. As they moved west and chose a location where they would build their houses, several requirements guided their decisions. Of course, they* needed to be near good water—water sufficient for themselves, their crops and their livestock. They needed land with large open areas that were free of rocks—not stony soil.

In the field of stony ground, there was only a very shallow soil layer on top of bedrock. The soil looked fertile from the surface, but there was not enough depth to sustain a root system or provide water. Jesus was saying that sometimes God's Word only makes a temporary impression on some people. Their hearts, like the stony places, may pay attention to what God is saying. Initially, they seem emotionally touched by His message and eager to learn more. But there is nothing deeply-rooted. As soon as temptation or oppositions come, their interest in religion withers away and dies.

Thorns—The word "thorns" is probably better translated weeds, since thorns grow on some of them. The root systems of some weeds grow very deep into the ground. Even when pulled out, some of the roots may remain. Unless the weeds are completely removed, they will soon grow and overtake any crop that has been planted.

Jesus was saying that some people listen to God's Word and actually know it is true. However, their hearts are like thorny ground because they are so absorbed with the pleasures and possessions of this world. These people may really enjoy the Bible and seem to want to obey what God says. However, they never bear fruit because they have allowed the things of this world (represented by the weeds with thorns) to take the place of God. They cannot come to the point of giving up these distractions in order to "seek first His kingdom."

Good Ground—The good ground refers to those who not only hear God's Word, but obey it. Jesus said that the good ground bears a crop—some 30, some 60, and some 100 times more than what was sown. He made it very clear that the evidence of good soil is the good crops it produces.

The crop Jesus was speaking of is spiritual—repentance toward God, faith toward the Lord Jesus Christ, holiness of life, good character, prayerfulness, humility, love, and spiritual-mindedness. These are obvious proofs that the seed of God's Word is effective in a person's heart.

Gr8-1: I've heard those verses many times before, but I've never really given a lot of thought to them. It's obvious that God wants us to be "growing crops" and "bearing fruit."

PHETI: I agree. The reason Jesus told this parable was to remind us that there is only one right way to respond to His Word. Only those with hearts of "good ground" will enter His Kingdom.

PHETI: On the way to school this morning, Dad and I talked about what Pastor Ryan said. Then Dad reminded me of what happened several summers ago when we were diving. He and I went on a boat dive with eight other divers to a coral reef off the coast of Maui, Hawaii. First, the dive master told the group to stay within sight of each other while exploring the reef. After he completed the instructions about what to do and not to do, we entered the water.

The reef was beautiful and huge! After exploring it for about 20 minutes, my dad realized that there were no other divers around us. I hadn't really noticed because I was looking at all the fish. He signaled to me to surface (we were about 45 feet down). When we reached the ocean's surface, there was no one in sight. There were no divers, no dive marker, and no boat—just vast, rolling waves in all directions.

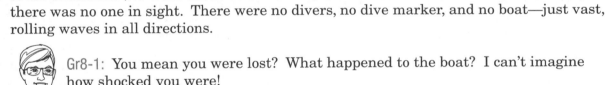

> **FACTOID**
>
> A mathematical possibility: Beginning with just 20 disciples, each converting just one person a year, and their converts doing the same . . . the growth would be like a mustard seed!
>
> - end of year 1—40 converts
> - end of year 5—640 converts
> - end of year 10—20,480 converts
> - end of year 15—655,360 converts
>
> The growth of the church in the first century A.D. confirmed the truth of Jesus' parable. The 120 disciples (Acts 1:15) grew to over 3,000 in just one day!

Gr8-1: You mean you were lost? What happened to the boat? I can't imagine how shocked you were!

PHETI: I've never seen my dad so scared. I was scared too. After floating on the surface for about five minutes, we saw the boat off in the distance. Fortunately, we had enough strength and air to make the swim back to the boat.

Gr8-1: Sounds like you thought the dive master's instructions were simply good advice rather than essential for survival. Was that your dad's point for reminding you of that experience?

PHETI: Well, he took full blame for ignoring the dive master's instruction to stick together. He knew it was important but hadn't taken it seriously. Because he didn't pay attention, he had put not only his own life, but also my life, in jeopardy. Dad said that we need to view God's Word as more than good advice. I should not think about my devotions as just a religious ritual that Christians are supposed to do. Instead, I should read my Bible and pray because it's essential to have God's wisdom as I live day to day.

PHETI: My Dad explained that God gives us His guidance at least three ways. They're important so I added them to my notes.

1. Commandments from God's Word. Dad said I should always remember that the best guidance I will ever receive comes right from the pages of the Bible. Usually God's expectations are very clear and direct. For example, in the Ten Commandments God leaves no doubt as to what He means. Jesus also made very clear and direct statements. When God speaks clearly about a subject, we have no doubt about what He means. And we have no option but obedience.

At other times we must rely on the principles of His Word to provide guidance. For example, my body is the temple of the Holy Spirit. Therefore, I should not endanger it with poor practices of health or safety. This is a conclusion I can draw from Scripture. I can also learn from the mistakes and triumphs of other people in the Bible. Their lives were meant to be examples for us.

2. Leadership from the Holy Spirit. According to John 16:13, the Holy Spirit has been sent to give us personal guidance. It's His job to lead me in agreement with God's Word. Every Christian needs to understand that the Holy Spirit is constantly present with us, teaching and convicting of sin, as well as conforming us to righteousness. He is always there to help us make the right decision.

3. Good advice from godly mentors and friends. The Bible often talks about the influence others have on us. In Psalm 1:1 we are told not to walk in the counsel of the ungodly. In Proverbs 13:20 Solomon said, "He who walks with wise men will be wise, but the companion of fools will be destroyed."

My dad and mom are always good sources of instruction. Pastors, youth ministers, teachers, and older friends can also be good sources for advice. But when I receive advice from friends, it is important that they are people who seek to obey God and His Word. Otherwise, their advice may be contrary to God's will for my life.

Gr8-1: It was great you had some time with your dad. You guys had quite a conversation!

PHETI: Yeah, it was fun to go to the Bible study and then talk about those things. I now am really committed to reading God's Word and praying. It's not something I should see as a chore. I need to know God's instructions for my survival.

Faith

His conception
I believe that my Saviour's conception was pure,
That His Father was God up above,
That His coming from glory will ever endure
As a message of infinite love.

His birth
I believe that my Saviour was born of a maid
Who was truly a virgin in fact,
Who, though troubled in spirit, would not be afraid.
Of this strange, and yet sanctified, act.

His life
I believe that my Saviour was true to His call
To exemplify God upon earth,
Though rejected so cruelly, to offer to all
His forgiveness, His healing, His worth.

His death
I believe that my Saviour was totally dead,
That He rested three days in the grave,
That He hung on the cross, that He suffered and bled,
That His blood is sufficient to save.

His resurrection
I believe that my Saviour arose from the tomb,
That He finished His work, as He said,
That He overcame death, with its terror and gloom,
That He offers us glory instead.

His ascension
I believe that my Saviour ascended on high,
Just as swift as a bird, and as free,
And that somewhere, with God, out beyond,
He's preparing a mansion for me.

His return
I believe that my Saviour will honor His word,
For He said He was coming again,
That the sound of the trumpet will be heard.
And I thrill as I listen. Amen!

–Alvy E. Ford

Parable of the Sower Summarize your findings.

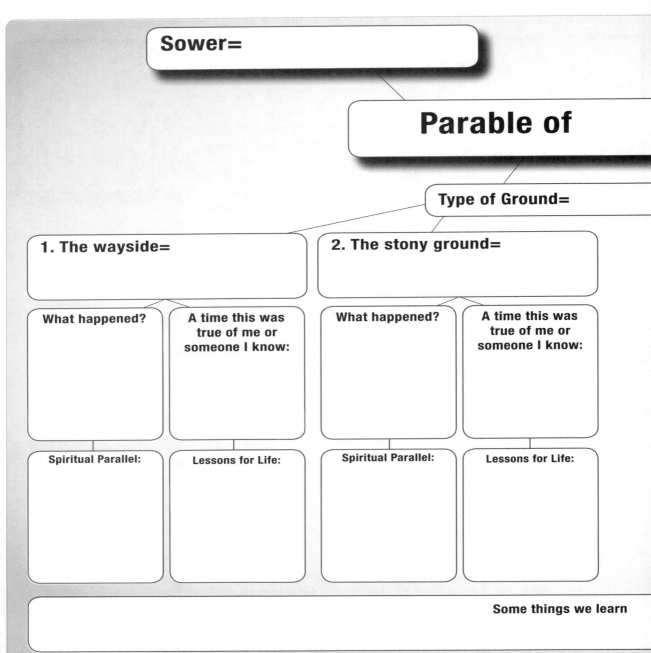

Sower=

Parable of

Type of Ground=

1. The wayside=

2. The stony ground=

What happened?	A time this was true of me or someone I know:	What happened?	A time this was true of me or someone I know:
Spiritual Parallel:	Lessons for Life:	Spiritual Parallel:	Lessons for Life:

Some things we learn

Seed=

the Sower

3. The thorny ground=

What happened?	A time this was true of me or someone I know:

Spiritual Parallel:	Lessons for Life:

4. The good ground=

What happened?	A time this was true of me or someone I know:

Spiritual Parallel:	Lessons for Life:

about the Kingdom of God:

Family Chatroom/Draw Near to God

Interact with your parents or another adult to find out how they have handled these situations.

1. A person I dearly loved seemed to grow distant and uncaring.

a) How I felt: _____

_____

b) What seemed to cause the problem: _____

_____

c) What was done to resolve it: _____

_____

2. I felt distanced from God—just seemed like my prayers went no higher than the ceiling, and Bible reading became a chore.

a) What seemed to cause the problem: _____

_____

b) What was done to resolve it: _____

_____

3. My advice to teens on how to keep a close relationship to the Lord:

a) _____

_____

_____

b) _____

_____

_____
Parent's Signature

Kingdom Facts

Record facts about the Kingdom of God that you have learned from studying the nine parables this week.

THE CHARACTER OF CHRIST

QUEST TRUTH

Jesus Christ possessed impeccable character demonstrated through His power and compassion. Believers are ordained to be conformed to His character as they set their minds on things above and seek to live in accordance with His commandments.

 QTee: Here we are again, Ginny! We're so sorry to bother you right now because we know you're studying for exams. But we are really upset! We messed up, and we've been feeling really bad. You said that if we ever needed to talk about something, you'd listen.

 IM4Him: It's about last weekend. You see, a bunch of kids threw a party, and we were invited. We both knew some of them, but most didn't attend our school.

 QTee: Everything started out okay, but it didn't stay that way; there weren't any parents chaperoning the party. After about an hour, things got out of hand. The language, drinking, and behavior were disgusting. Some of us wanted to leave, especially Sarah and me, but we didn't. We felt like we were trapped!

 IM4Him: We didn't want to be associated with what the others were doing, but we were too embarrassed to call our parents. So we stuck around and made the best of it until some others were leaving. Now we both feel awful. By staying, we feel like we supported what they were doing. We feel really guilty.

 QTee: Yeah, we just didn't stand up for what we believe. We're not sure if there is any way we can undo what's already happened. And we sure don't want to make the same mistake twice.

 2B4Givn: Too bad about what happened, but I can tell you why you were so uncomfortable. Your character was put to the test. When you have the Holy Spirit living inside you, it's natural to feel uncomfortable in a place that's out of sync with His character. Let me explain.

Have you noticed people wearing those WWJD bracelets? Of course, the message is a good one. There's nothing wrong with asking ourselves: What would Jesus do? Christians are challenged to follow Christ's example and to imitate God in the way we live (Ephesians 5:1-2). But what happens when we are forced to take the message beyond a bracelet and past a fad? What happens when the character of Jesus is put to the test in the way we live?

IM4Him: That's exactly what happened! We both have the WWJD bracelets. At the party we should have done more than wear a bracelet.

 2B4Givn: Obviously, God's Spirit convicted you because you were part of an activity that dishonored Him. That's a clear indication that you desire to follow the Lord. Although you didn't actually participate in what was going on, you knew that your presence would indicate agreement with their actions. Not only did that make you uncomfortable, but it also made you realize the need for greater strength in your own character.

 IM4Him: You've nailed it! We should have had better sense than to go in the first place. And after we were there, we didn't know how to handle the situation.

 2B4Givn: That reminds me of a story Dad once told me. As a little boy, his father attended a huge church in downtown Chicago. After the music and the preaching, the ushers took up the offering—this was the fun part. Wait, I have it in my journal file.

FILE SHARING

Twelve men with solemn faces and long coats would march in lock-step down the main aisle of the church carrying heavy brass offering plates. These were not just any men. They were some of the most well-known business and professional leaders in the city. One of them was a man named Frank Loesch. Although he looked like an average sort of guy, he was a Chicago legend; he was the man who stood up to the notorious gangster Al Capone.

During the prohibition years, Al Capone ruled Chicago. Even the police and the FBI were afraid to oppose him. But Frank Loesch, a Christian businessman, organized the Chicago Crime Commission—a group of citizens committed to seeing Capone convicted. Frank Loesch's life was in constant danger during those months, but he never backed down. Finally, they won an important case against Capone. It was the beginning of the end for Capone's iron rule in Chicago. Within a few months, Al Capone was convicted of tax evasion and sent to jail. Frank Loesch had risked his life to live out his faith.

Every Sunday, when the offering was being taken, Granddad would poke Dad in the side and point to Frank Loesch. As a Chicago businessman, Granddad was also often threatened by Al Capone. He wanted his son to see a man who lived according to his Christian principles.

QTee: I see your point. It's easy to talk about what we believe, but it's a lot harder to actually live out our commitments. It's just hard when you have to stand up to people who know you.

2B4Givn: That's why Jesus did more than just teach about what was good or what we should do. He also showed us, by the way He lived His life, how to do good and honor God. There are five miracles that clearly illustrate the character of our Lord: quieting the storm, casting demons into swine, healing a woman, raising Jairus' daughter, and healing the blind and mute. I want you both to review each of these, then we'll meet online again in about an hour. What do you say?

IM4Him: Sounds good to me. Those are some of my favorite miracles in the Bible. See you both in an hour.

PROCESSING

2B4Givn: Okay, we're back. I'll take the first one, but you two have to take the others. Here goes.

Miracle 1: Quieting the storm. This story is about crossing the Sea of Galilee. The eastern shore is bordered by a steep section of hills. It is not unusual for a cold wind to shoot through the gaps and collide with the warm air, creating a particularly dangerous weather pattern.

As Jesus slept in the boat, a waterspout emerged, and the disciples found themselves threatened with destruction. Fearing that the boat could easily be capsized, the disciples cried out, "Master, Master, we are perishing!"

Jesus responded in two ways. First, He rebuked the wind and the sea. Immediately, they became calm. Second, He turned to the disciples and asked, "Where is your faith?" Can you imagine the look on their faces? One minute they were terrified that the boat would be capsized, and the next minute the sea was as calm as glass. Some of them were former fishermen who had been on the lake in the midst of storms. They knew how powerless sailors are in facing natural forces. Though their faith was weak, they did the right thing in turning to Jesus for help.

I think we can learn some lessons from this miracle. When we're in a difficult situation (even one of our own making), Jesus is compassionate. The disciples were terrified, but Jesus brought immediate calmness and control. Even during tough times, God will still take care of us. This is another clear illustration that Jesus is truly God.

QTee: I like that application. Already I see how we could have trusted God more in our situation. Let me try the next one.

Miracle 2: Healing a demoniac. This was not the first time Jesus performed an exorcism. The Gospel writers recorded this story for at least a couple of reasons. First, this story involves multiple possession, not just a single demon. Second, this miracle involves earthly creatures other than humans.

The story began as the man fell before Jesus and the demons confessed Him to be the "Son of the Most High God." The demons' name was Legion, indicating that a whole battle division (thousands of demons) inhabited the man. In other words, Jesus was engaged in a major battle. He was outnumbered but not overmatched.

The demons asked to be sent into a herd of pigs rather than into the Abyss—the pit, the underworld, the prison where demons are sent. At Jesus' command, the demons departed to enter the pigs. Immediately, the pigs panicked and ran over the edge of a steep bank and into the water, where they drowned. Word spread fast that the demon-possessed man was healed and the herd of swine had jumped off a cliff to their death.

Because of His power over the spirit world, the local people were afraid, and they asked Jesus to leave the area. Jesus then instructed the man to stay behind and tell what God had done. Making the application is sort of difficult. How about some help?

2B4Givn: Once again, Jesus had shown His compassion. But there is another important lesson that we can learn from this story. Look at what Luke said in 8:38—"Now the man from whom the demons had departed begged Him that he might be with Him. But Jesus sent him away, saying, 'Return to your own house, and tell what great things God has done for you.'"

Remember, not everyone is called to a mission field far from home. Jesus wants those who have experienced His goodness to first tell those in their own family and hometown. Some are called to go; others are called to stay; but all are called to be witnesses for Christ.

> **FACTOID**
>
> The Sea of Galilee is more than 690 feet below sea level. To the north, Mount Hermon rises to 9,200 feet above sea level. From May to October, strong winds sweep through the surrounding gorges, causing extremely sudden and violent storms.

IM4Him: It makes me think that we still have a responsibility to share Christ with others we know. Okay, I have the third miracle.

Miracle 3: Healing a woman. As this story opened, Jesus was in the midst of a huge crowd. Standing nearby was a synagogue ruler named Jairus. Everyone knew him. As Jesus approached, he bowed and asked Jesus to come to his house where his only daughter, a 12 year old, was near death. Rescuing her required quick action.

As Jesus headed toward Jairus's house, another person needed healing— a woman who had suffered from a blood disease for 12 years. No physician had been able to help her. Obviously, she did not want public attention. So, hidden in the crowd, she approached Jesus from behind and softly touched the hem of His garment. Immediately she was healed.

Jesus stopped, turned to the crowd and asked, "Who touched Me?" Both Jairus and Peter were shocked. Jairus wanted Jesus to hurry and help his daughter. Peter couldn't believe what Jesus asked. The crowd was so large that it was impossible to know who had bumped into Jesus.

But Jesus knew the touch was not just physical, but a touch that pleaded for help. Jesus wanted to know who had exercised enough faith to seek His touch—a touch that resulted in healing. The woman realized that Jesus knew what she had done. With great fear she stepped forward to identify herself. She fell on her knees before Him and told her story. To her surprise, Jesus did not rebuke her. Instead, He praised her faith and encouraged her to go in peace.

I included Jesus' compassion as one lesson to remember—first for Jairus's daughter, then for the woman who had touched Him. Knowing that the woman had acted in faith, He wanted to encourage her. In the midst of a huge crowd, Jesus was sensitive to the needs of a single individual.

QTee: That's an encouragement to us to be sensitive in our approach to others, as well as to focus on them as individuals. I also noticed that the fourth miracle was a continuation of the story related to Jairus's plea for help.

Miracle 4: Raising Jairus's daughter. Can you imagine the frustration Jairus felt as he waited while Jesus talked to the woman? All he could think about was how sick his daughter was and how important it was for Jesus to reach her as quickly as possible.

QTee: Then things got worse. A servant from Jairus's house told him it was too late and that Jesus didn't need to be bothered—his daughter had already died. Jesus comforted the synagogue ruler, telling him not to fear but to believe.

At the house, Jesus allowed only the parents, Peter, John, and James to enter the room where the corpse lay. Mourners had already gathered outside to express their grief. Jesus instructed them to be quiet, for the girl was not dead but sleeping. Immediately the crowd of mourners mocked Him with laughter.

Once inside the room, Jesus took the girl's hand and told her to get up. There were no potions, no magic, and no appeal to special extraterrestrial powers. Jesus simply touched her, and immediately the girl sat up. Her parents were amazed. The promise that Jesus had made to Jairus was now fulfilled.

2B4Givn: I love reading that miracle. Jesus was so tender with Jairus and his daughter. Also, He was not affected by the negative remarks of the crowd. You both have done a great job, but I would like to take the last one.

Miracle 5: Healing two blind men and a mute demoniac. In rapid succession Jesus performed two more miracles. As He made His way to Capernaum, two blind men begged for mercy from the Son of David, a name meaning "the expected Messiah." In response to their faith, Jesus touched their eyes to heal them but warned them not to tell about their experience—a warning they promptly ignored. While they were leaving, a mute, demon-possessed man was brought to Jesus for healing. The observers recognized Jesus' power with the response, "Nothing like this has ever happened in Israel!"

In all the miracles, Jesus demonstrated different aspects of His character. He showed compassion, love, sensitivity, the willingness to confront unbelievers, and patience. The strength of Jesus' character was evident in everything He did.

IM4Him: You're right, I was pretty familiar with those miracles. Still, I needed the reminder that they illustrate how we need to live out what we say we believe.

2B4Givn: That's why I wanted you to review them. Although you didn't participate in the activities, your failure to leave the party told others that you were okay with what was going on. You said you didn't want to make the same mistake twice. Can I give you a couple of tips that might help?

QTee: Yes, please! That's why we contacted you. We knew that you had probably faced this sort of thing before.

 2B4Givn: I have. That's why I think these two tips will help you.

Tip 1: The past will pursue you. (Just don't give up.) This is probably one of the most difficult lessons to learn for people who are trying to change the way they've lived. Although you may want to forget what happened in the past, others won't. They will constantly remind you of how you used to talk, act, and think. Every time you try to do the right thing, someone will be there to remind you of your past failures.

The Apostle Paul could relate to that. As a young man, Paul zealously persecuted Christians. Then one day he encountered Jesus Christ and became a believer himself. At first none of the other Christians would believe what happened to him. Eventually they grew to trust him. In the same way, it requires a consistent testimony over time for people to know that you've really changed.

Don't let your own past discourage you or defeat you. Even though others may try to remind you of what happened, determine that you are going to do what's right in the future. Given time, you will earn the respect of others for the decisions you make.

Tip 2: God will make a way, even in the most difficult situation. One day you will find yourself in another compromising situation. This time you'll be prepared. When the next difficult situation comes, immediately ask God to provide a way out.

Remember, God's promise in 1 Corinthians 10:13 is "No temptation has overtaken you except such as is common to man; but God is faithful, who will not allow you to be tempted beyond what you are able, but with the temptation will also make the way of escape, that you may be able to bear it." We cannot always handle difficult situations in our own strength. Be calm and look for the way that God has provided to deliver you from the situation.

I hope this helps. I know how both of you feel—I've been there too. Just keep studying the life of Jesus and looking for ways to model His character in your life.

Family Chatroom/Learning from the Experiences of Others

Discuss the questions with your parents. Be sure you have their permission to share their responses with your class.

1. What experience/s have you had in which you were caught in a situation that was in opposition to your beliefs about what is the right way to live?

_____

_____

_____

_____

2. What did you do to try to handle the situation? _____

_____

_____

_____

_____

3. What was the outcome? _____

_____

_____

_____

_____

4. What should I, and other teens, do if caught in similar situations?

_____

_____

_____

_____

_____
Parent's Signature

QuestFile 17.2

The Miracles Summarize the presentations on the five miracles of Jesus.

Characteristics of Christ   Lessons to be Learned

Calming the Storm

_____   _____
_____   _____
_____   _____

Healing a Demoniac

_____   _____
_____   _____
_____   _____

Healing a Woman

_____   _____
_____   _____
_____   _____

Raising Jairus's Daughter

_____   _____
_____   _____
_____   _____

Healing Two Blind Men and a Mute Demoniac

_____   _____
_____   _____
_____   _____

AN UNFINISHED BOOK

 PHETI: Getting us all together online is a great idea. With everyone's schedule so packed, it's almost impossible otherwise.

 IM4Him: I agree. By reviewing for our exams this way I'll probably remember the information better.

 Gr8-1: I think it will be fun. So, tonight we said we're going to review for Bible. How do you want to start?

 IM4Him: I think we need to do what Mr. Gifford suggested. He said we needed to have a "big picture" understanding of what we've learned so far about the life of Jesus Christ. Why don't we take turns explaining each of the chapters?

>
> ## FACTOID
>
> In 1985 a boat was unearthed from the mud after a drought had exposed the seabed of the Sea of Galilee. The boat was dated to the time of Christ. It could hold up to 15 men, and four men were required to row it. A similar boat could have easily accommodated Jesus and His disciples on their trip from Capernaum to Gadara.

QTee: That's a good idea. I'll start with the first chapter. That week was called "Before Time Began." We learned that Jesus Christ is God and that He existed before time began. We studied the message Paul preached to the Greeks on Mars Hill in Acts 17. Of course, the main point of his sermon was to answer the question, "Who is God?" As a result, we learned that the same facts true about God were also true about His Son, Jesus Christ. According to John 1:1, Jesus Christ was "in the beginning." He was not only perfect man, but perfect God. Tyler, why don't you take the next chapter.

PHETI: I'll never forget Week 2. That's when we talked about explaining God's plan of redemption using only the Old Testament! At first I thought it was impossible. But then we learned that most of biblical prophecy concerns either the First Coming of Jesus Christ (including His ministry, death, resurrection, and ascension) or the Second Coming of Jesus Christ (including His reign on earth and His Kingdom in heaven). I realized that it is impossible to fully understand the life of Jesus Christ without studying the Old Testament. Tim, what about the next chapter?

Gr8-1: In the next chapter we asked the question "Do things just happen?" That's something we all think about as things happen to us. Do they happen by accident, or are they a part of a master plan? We learned in this chapter that the Bible teaches that history is HIS STORY. Even as far back as the first century, the Apostle Paul reminded us that the birth of Jesus Christ occurred exactly according to God's plan. We studied what it meant by "the fullness of time" mentioned in Galatians 4. God has a plan, and it is unfolding right before our very eyes. Sarah, you're next.

IM4Him: Before I review the next chapter, did you notice something interesting about these first three weeks? We didn't talk about the birth of Jesus Christ. Whenever we've talked about the life of Christ in Sunday School, we always started with His birth in the manger.

Gr8-1: You're right. But remember what Mr. Gifford said. We need to understand that because Jesus is God, He existed before time began and that He is part of God's plan as revealed in the Old Testament. Once we understand those facts, we are ready for the story of His birth.

IM4Him: Let me review the next two lessons together. In Week 4 we learned about the incarnation and why it is foundational to our faith and salvation. Only someone who is God, as well as man, could pay the infinite price of people's sin. That's the true importance of the story of Jesus' birth. In Week 5 we talked about what Jesus was like when He was a 12-year-old boy. Although the Bible provides very little information about Jesus' childhood, we know that He amazed the religious leaders with His understanding of the Scriptures. We also talked about the obedience He showed to his parents. His life is a good example to us in developing our mind, body, social skills, and spiritual life. Megan, it's your turn.

QTee: In Week 6 we fast-forwarded almost 20 years. The Bible does not discuss what Jesus did between the time He was 12 years old and His baptism by John the Baptist. This was the beginning of His public, three-year ministry. It was also the first of three times that God spoke from heaven confirming Jesus as His Son. Following His baptism, we studied the incredible way Jesus resisted the temptations of Satan. Okay Tyler, what was in the next chapter?

PHETI: I think one of the most interesting things in Week 7 was learning that Jesus' disciples were all just ordinary people. I'm sure that, as teenagers, they never dreamed they would one day be a part of a select group to travel with the Messiah. Mr. Gifford reminded us that Jesus is always looking for people—of all ages—who are willing to faithfully follow Him. Your turn, Tim.

Gr8-1: This was really an interesting lesson. We talked about whether or not there might be more than one plan of salvation and that what Jesus said might not be true. That was really Nicodemus's question when he asked Jesus if He had been sent from God. Jesus made it very clear that He is the only path to salvation. The part I liked best was the challenge from C. S. Lewis—We must decide: Jesus is either a liar, a lunatic, or truly Lord.

 IM4Him: Since Weeks 9 through 11 all dealt with Jesus' ministry, I will review all of them. In Week 9 we learned that ministry is not reserved just for pastors and church staff. Jesus expects each of us to share in the responsibilities of spreading the gospel.

During Week 10 we learned that Jesus' ministry was constantly under attack from the Jewish religious leaders. But I thought it was interesting that not all of the attacks came from just the Jewish leaders. Once the criticism came from the disciples of John the Baptist, and often it came from Jesus' own disciples. However, no matter how severe the attacks, Jesus continued His ministry. It was a good reminder to me that when we are trying to do the right thing, we will often suffer criticism and unjust treatment.

In Week 11 we learned how the Pharisees criticized Jesus because He did not honor the Sabbath the way they thought He should. Matter of fact, their anger was so intense against Him that they accused Him of being from Satan. The Pharisees refused to accept Jesus as the Son of God. As a result, Jesus took His ministry to the common people.

 QTee: In the next lesson we learned about the longest sermon of Jesus recorded in the Gospels. In the Sermon on the Mount (Matthew 5–7) Jesus spoke directly to the masses about their relationship with God. He described the lifestyle of a believer—one who desires to be a part of His Kingdom. He explained that happiness only comes when we live according to the principles that God has established. On to Week 13!

 PHETI: It seems to me that the remaining lessons, 13-17, all deal with the same theme. Based on various miracles and teachings, they all relate to how a believer should live.

 Gr8-1: It looks like you're right. I hadn't noticed that before. Why don't you go ahead and summarize the remaining lessons.

FACTOID

Nature forms us;
sin deforms us;
His Word informs us;
the Holy Spirit conforms us;
and Christ transforms us.
PTL!

PHETI: No problem! The focus of Week 13 was prayer. Prayer is communication with God. By providing the Lord's Prayer, Jesus gave a model for how we should pray. First, our prayers should both begin and end with praise to God. Then we should pray or our needs, our forgiveness and our protection. Prayer should not be an afterthought for Christians. It should be a natural part of life.

In Week 14 we talked about Life 101. We studied the parable of the two builders (Matthew 7) and the parable of the blind leading the blind (Luke 6). The point of this chapter is that we must live out our faith daily. Christianity is a way of life. Before I try to instruct others, I must make sure that my own life is in harmony with what Jesus teaches.

What we need to do to have more faith was the subject of Week 15. We studied the miracles of Jesus recorded in Matthew 8 and Luke 7. Mr. Gifford told us that Jesus performed these miracles because He cared about others. But he said there was another reason—Jesus wanted His followers to grow in their faith. We learned that there are two principles we must follow if we want to have more faith. First, we need to be intentional about doing the will of God right from the start. Second, we must surrender to God on a day-to-day basis.

The study of the parables of the Kingdom, in Week 16, was very interesting. In these parables, Jesus helps us understand the relationship between our daily lives and our spiritual lives. We were reminded that God's Word provides good counsel. If we fail to follow God's advice, we will make the wrong decisions in life.

 QTee: Time out. I just want everyone to know, before Tyler reviews Week 17, that this was the chapter that had the greatest impact on me this year. I've been in some situations that made me very uncomfortable. This lesson really helped me to know what to do the next time that happens.

PHETI: I agree—Week 17 was very practical. Our character is put to the test every day. This lesson challenged us to model the character of the Lord in our reactions. We should not be defeated or discouraged by our past failures. When we're faced with difficult situations in the future, God will make a way.

 IM4Him: You're right! These final five lessons all relate to how we live. I'm now beginning to better understand the big picture. Jesus' life and ministry are the fulfillment of hundreds of Old Testament prophecies. He is the Messiah of the Jews who became the Savior of all who believe in His name. After we receive Him as our Savior, we have the responsibility to live as He teaches us through His Word.

QUESTFILE 18.1

Understanding the Big Picture Complete the study guide for the chapter assigned to you.

Week number: _____ Title: _____

1. Where does this lesson fit on the review timeline presented in class?

   _____ Jesus' existence before the beginning of time

   _____ Jesus' birth and boyhood

   _____ Jesus' preparation for ministry

   _____ Jesus' message and ministry

2. List three things you learned about the life of Christ from this lesson.

   1) _____

   2) _____

   3) _____

3. What was the most important personal lesson you learned from this week's study? _____

   _____

   _____

4. List five questions or facts that you believe are so important that they should be a part of your final exam:

   1) _____

   2) _____

   3) _____

   4) _____

   5) _____

Understanding the Big Picture Complete the study guide for the chapter assigned to you.

Week number: _____ Title: _____

1. Where does this lesson fit on the review timeline presented in class?

    _____ Jesus' existence before the beginning of time

    _____ Jesus' birth and boyhood

    _____ Jesus' preparation for ministry

    _____ Jesus' message and ministry

2. List three things you learned about the life of Christ from this lesson.

    1) _____

    2) _____

    3) _____

3. What was the most important personal lesson you learned from this week's study? _____

    _____

    _____

4. List five questions or facts that you believe are so important that they should be a part of your final exam:

    1) _____

    2) _____

    3) _____

    4) _____

    5) _____

QUESTFILE 18.3

Commitment Counts Your paper will not be seen by anyone except you. Your honest answers will allow God to work as you become more conformed to the image of Christ.

The one truth from this course that has been most important to me is . . . _____

_____

_____

An area of Christ-likeness which I feel more confident in handling now is . . . _____

_____

_____

The area of Christ-likeness that needs most improvement in how I handle things is . . .

_____

_____

The biggest obstacle to my improving this area is . . . _____

_____

_____

Some things I want to work on are . . . _____

_____

_____

I want to commit myself to being conformed to Christ's image.   Yes ❑   No ❑

If yes, complete the next page. ➞

Commitment to Becoming More Christ-like

B Based on the challenges presented in this course, I am willing to commit myself to conforming to the image of Christ. I understand that this includes my commitment to mature choices, a right attitude, and conscientious actions based on God's Word.

_____
Signature

_____
Date

That I may know Him and the power of His resurrection, and the fellowship of His sufferings, being conformed to His death. I press toward the goal for the prize of the upward call of God in Christ Jesus.

–Philippians 3:10 & 14

SCRIPTUREQUEST

GLOSSARY

MAPS

SCRITUREQUEST

| DAY 1 | DAY 2 | DAY 3 | DAY 4 | DAY 5 | FAVORITES/NOTES |

Week 1: Before Time Began

☐ John 1:1–5,9-14

☐ Job 38:1-21

☐ Hebrews 1:1-10

☐ Colossians 1:9-23; 2:2-3,8-10

☐ Isaiah 40:12-31

Week 2: The Old in the New

☐ Ephesians 1

☐ Romans 10:8-17

☐ Psalm 22:1-8,14-19

☐ Isaiah 53:1-10

☐ Jeremiah 23:3-8

Week 3: In the Fullness of Time

☐ Matthew 1:1-17

☐ Luke 3:23b-38

☐ Luke 1:5-17

☐ Psalm 139:1-18

☐ Isaiah 7:14; 9:6-7; 11:1-5; 42:1-12

DAY 1	DAY 2	DAY 3	DAY 4	DAY 5	FAVORITES/NOTES

Week 4: A Child Is Born

☐ Matthew 1:5-25 ☐ Luke 1:26-56 ☐ Luke 2:1-20 ☐ Philippians 2:1-16 ☐ Luke 2:21-39

_____

_____

_____

_____

_____

Week 5: A Model Child

☐ Matthew 2:1-12 ☐ Matthew 2:13-23 ☐ Luke 2:40-52 ☐ Ephesians 6:1-3; Colossians 3:20-24 ☐ Proverbs 1:8-9; 3:1-2; 6:20-24; 23:22-25

_____

_____

_____

_____

_____

_____

Week 6: A Voice in the Desert

☐ Isaiah 40:3-11; Malachi 3:1; 4:5-6; Mark 1:1-8 ☐ Luke 1:5-25,57-80; Matthew 3:1-12 ☐ Matthew 11:2-18; Luke 3:1-13; John 1:19-34 ☐ Matthew 3:13-17; Mark 1:9-15; Luke 3:15-22 ☐ Matthew 14:1-12; Mark 6:17-29; John 3:22-30

_____

_____

_____

_____

_____

DAY 1	DAY 2	DAY 3	DAY 4	DAY 5	FAVORITES/NOTES

Week 7: Calling Disciples

Matthew 4:1-11; Mark 1:12-15

Luke 4:1-13; Hebrews 4:14-16

Mark 1:16-20; Mark 2:13-14; Mark 3:13-19

Matthew 4:18-25; Luke 5:1-11; John 1:35-51

Luke 2:21-39

Week 8: A Call to Worship

John 2:13-25

John 3:1-21

John 3:22-36

John 4:1-42

John 4:43-54

Week 9: Directions of Ministry

Matthew 4:13-25; Acts 10:36-43

Luke 4:14-44; 5:1-11

Mark 1:14b-15,21-34,35-39

1 Kings 17:9-16; 2 Kings 5:14; Psalm 34:15-22

Isaiah 61:1-2, 6; 9:1-2; Psalm 147:1-7

DAY 1	DAY 2	DAY 3	DAY 4	DAY 5	FAVORITES/NOTES

Week 10: Jesus Performs Miracles

☐ Matthew 8:1-4; Mark 1:40-45; Luke 5:12-16

☐ Mark 2:1-12

☐ Matthew 9:1-8; Luke 5:17-26

☐ Matthew 9:9-17; Mark 2:15-22

☐ Luke 5:29-39; Hosea 6:6

_____
_____
_____
_____
_____
_____
_____

Week 11: The Beginning of Conflicts

☐ John 5:1-47

☐ Matthew 12:1-8; Mark 2:23-28; Luke 6:1-5; 1 Samuel 21:1-6

☐ Matthew 12:9-21; Mark 3:1-6; Luke 6:6-11

☐ Matthew 12:22-29; Mark 3:7-12; Isaiah 42:1-4

☐ Proverbs 8:6-8; 11:11-13; 12:22; 13:3; 17:27-28; 19:9

_____
_____
_____
_____
_____
_____

Week 12: Sermon on the Mount

☐ Matthew 5:1-16; Luke 6:20-26

☐ Matthew 5:17-48; 6:19-34

☐ Matthew 6:5-18

☐ Luke 6:27-49

☐ Matthew 7:1-29

_____
_____
_____
_____

DAY 1	DAY 2	DAY 3	DAY 4	DAY 5	FAVORITES/NOTES

Week 13: Practicing Prayer

☐ Matthew 6:5-15; Luke 11:1-4

☐ Matthew 7:7-11; Luke 11:5-13

☐ Luke 18:9-14; James 1:17; 4:3; Psalm 145:18-19

☐ 1 John 5:14-15; John 15:7; James 4:3; Psalm 66:16-20; John 14:12-17

☐ 1 Thessalonians 5:17-18; 1 John 3:2; Mark 11:24; Philippians 4:6-7

Week 14: Teaching in Parables

☐ Matthew 7:3-14; Luke 6:39-42; Titus 3:1-8

☐ Matthew 7:15-20; Luke 6:43-45

☐ Matthew 7:24-27; Luke 6:46-49; John 14:15,23-26

☐ James 1:22-25; 1 John 2:3-6; 5:1-3

☐ Psalm 103:17-21; 119:1-16,57-64

Week 15: The Power of Faith

☐ Luke 7:1-16; Matthew 8:5-13

☐ Luke 7:17-35; Matthew 11:1-19

☐ Matthew 11:20-30

☐ Luke 7:36–8:3

☐ Matthew 12:22-50; Mark 3:20-35; Luke 8:19-21

DAY 1	DAY 2	DAY 3	DAY 4	DAY 5	FAVORITES/NOTES

Week 16: The Kingdom of God

☐	☐	☐	☐	☐
Matthew 13:1-8; Mark 4:1-12; Luke 8:4-10	Matthew 13:18-23; Mark 4:13-20; Luke 8:11-15	Mark 4:26-29; Matthew 13:24-30,36-43	Matthew 13:31-35, 44-50; Mark 4:30-34; Luke 13:18-21	Matthew 13:9-17, 51-52; Mark 4:21-25; Luke 8:16-18

Week 17: The Character of Christ

☐	☐	☐	☐	☐
Matthew 8:18,23-27; Mark 4:35-41; Luke 8:22-25	Matthew 8:28–9:1a; Mark 5:1-20; Luke 8:26-39	Matthew 9: 20-22; Mark 5:24b-34; Luke 8:42b-48	Matthew 9:1b, 18-19,23-26; Mark 5:21-24a,35-43; Luke 8:40-42,49-56	Matthew 9:27-38; Romans 1:1-7; Philippians 3:8-14

A

Abyss—the pit, the underworld, hell, a place reserved for Satan and his demons. (17)

adoration—the act of adoring, worship, giving honor, praise, glorifying. (13)

adultery—sexual relationships with someone other than a spouse. (12)

alms—money and material goods given to help the poor. (12)

Anno Domini—A.D. meaning "year of our Lord." It marks the time after Christ's birth. Its opposite is B.C. meaning "before Christ." (1)

annunciation—the announcement of Jesus' birth made by the angels. (3) (4)

ask—to request, to petition. Christians are to ask God for their needs and the needs of others as they pray. (13)

attribute—characteristic that is inherent in one's nature. (1)

B

baptism—immersion in water to show the burial, resurrection and walk in new life of a believer; an ordinance, ritual or sacrament of the church; baptism of the Spirit refers to being indwelt by the Holy Spirit at salvation. (6)

Bar mitzvah—son of the commandment; when a Jewish boy turns 13 years of age and is expected to take on adult religious duty and responsibility. (5)

Beatitudes—Jesus' statements related to "blessed or happy are" that define the standard for believers in the Kingdom of heaven in contrast to the Pharisees' distortion of the Law. (12)

Beelzebub—literally, "lord of flies" or "lord of filth"; regarded as the prince of demons—another name for Satan. (11)

Before Christ—B.C. meaning "before Christ." It marks the time before Christ's birth. Its opposite is A.D. meaning "year of our Lord." (1)

belief—a mental agreement that something is true; in a spiritual sense belief must lead to commitment to Christ which demonstrates itself in a changed life. (8) (15)

blaspheme—to show disrespect to God, to claim powers that only God possesses. (10) (11)

blind—inability to see, in a spiritual sense—not understanding, refusing to listen and obey, not accepting the truth. (14)

born again—to enter God's family through faith in Christ and the entrance of the Holy Spirit into your life. (8)

C

centurion—a Roman military officer responsible for 100 soldiers. (15)

conception—the beginning of life when a sperm and an ovum are united. (4)

condemned—to be judged guilty and deserving of punishment; In salvation Jesus removes the condemnation for our sin and makes us righteous before God. (8)

confession—agreeing with God as to your sin; admitting to others your wrongdoing, openly professing the name of Christ. (13)

consolation—an encouragement or expression of sympathy during a time of mourning or sorrow. (4)

covenant—an absolute, unbreakable promise; God, who cannot lie or break a promise, made several covenants between Himself and His people. (8)

create—to make from nothing. (1)

D

debt—something owed; another term used for sin. (13)

Decapolis—"ten cities"; the area east of the Sea of Galilee. (17)

demons—fallen angels thrown from heaven during Lucifer's (Satan's) rebellion who now inhabit the earth and work on behalf of Satan. (9) (15) (17)

doctrine—an organized set of principles or teachings about a subject, as in the doctrine of angels. (4)

draught—what is drawn together, for example, fish drawn up in a net. (9)

E

eternal—everlasting, forever, infinite, always in existence; without limits of time. (1)

exorcism—the removal of demons from an individual. (17)

express image—exact duplicate; visible representation of who God is. (1)

F

faith—a belief that leads to action, trust, an absolute assurance that what God says is true; the substance of things hoped for, evidence of things not seen. (8) (15)

fasting—voluntarily refusing to eat for a period of time in order to focus on spiritual matters. (10)

Feast of Unleavened Bread—a reminder of how God spared Israel and brought them out of the land of Egypt. (5)

Feast of Harvest—a demonstration of gratitude to God for the grain He had provided in the fields. (5)

Feast of Ingathering—a thanksgiving for the final harvest of the year. (5)

fool—a scorner; a thoughtless, reckless person; a person who does not think through the consequences of his actions or beliefs. (12)

forgiveness—erasing the account of wrongdoing, to not remember sins, to not seek revenge, to consider the penalty or debt paid-in-full. (13) (15)

friend—a person with whom you have a close, caring relationship; Jesus is the Friend of sinners in that He laid down His life in order to make a way for them to come to God. (10)

fullness of time—the perfect time for Christ to enter the world in accordance with God's plan. (3)

G

Gadara—a city on the eastern bank of the Sea of Galilee where a wild demoniac was healed. (17)

Gerasenes/Gergesenes—another name for the area on the eastern bank of the Sea of Galilee. (17)

gospel—good news. Gospel refers particularly to the good news of Christ—His death, resurrection, and offer of salvation to all who believe. (9)

grace—the undeserved favor of God in which He acts for the benefit of mankind. (8) (9)

H

hallowed—all holy, in complete fullness, opposite to vanity or taking the Lord's name in vain. (13)

harmony of the gospels—the effort to synchronize the events and details of the four Gospel accounts of the life of Christ. (9)

hyperbole—a language structure in which an over exaggeration is used in order to make a point. For example, John says that if everything about Christ had been written, even the skies could not contain the scrolls. (14)

hypocrite—a person whose words do not match his or her behavior; a person who pretends to be religious. (12) (13)

I

immaculate—completely pure; immaculate conception refers to the fact that Jesus Christ was conceived by the Holy Spirit and had no human father. (4)

Immanuel—the name given Jesus Christ that means "God with us." Same as Emmanuel. (3)

impeccable—completely without sin or error; only Christ lived an impeccable life. (4) (7)

incarnation—"in the flesh"; the doctrine that Christ as God's Son came to earth clothed in flesh as the perfect God-Man. (4)

infanticide—the killing of infants such as the "slaughter of innocents" ordered by Herod following the birth of Christ. (5)

intentional—doing something on purpose or with intent. (15)

intercession—praying for the needs of others, particularly toward the accomplishment of God's will. Intercessory prayer usually involves commitment of long periods of time to pray for defined needs. (13)

J

Jesus—the name of God's Son as announced to Mary, meaning Savior. (3)

jot—the smallest letter of the Hebrew alphabet. (12)

justification—giving reasons, offering amends; an act of God in which individuals are declared without sin because of the work of Jesus Christ that makes the forgiveness of sins possible. (15)

K

Kingdom of God—also written as the Kingdom of heaven, referring to the rule of God on earth first as a spiritual kingdom in the hearts of believers and ultimately, at the Second Coming of Christ, as an actual physical kingdom. (6) (16)

knock—to seek entrance, to rap on a door. Christians are to knock at the heart of God as they seek Him. (13)

L

Legion—the name used to refer to the demons residing in the two men of Gadara that were sent into a herd of 2,000 pigs. A legion was an army division containing thousands, usually 6,000 men. (17)

leaven—a fermented yeast that causes bread to rise; used in Scripture to illustrate influence that can permeate throughout the whole. (16)

leprosy—a contagious disease that causes ulcers on the body and progresses to loss of sensation and destruction of body tissues. (10)

Levi—one of the sons of Israel (Jacob); the tribe of Israel responsible for the Temple and worship procedures. (4)

lie—to misrepresent the truth, to deceive, to twist or pervert the truth. (11)

lineage—the family line extending back through parents, grandparents, etc. (3)

Lord's Day—Sunday, the first day of the week, when most Christians attend church and worship God. This day changed from the Jewish Sabbath, Saturday, which was consecrated to the Lord. (11)

Lord's Prayer—the model for prayer taught by Jesus during the Sermon on the Mount. (13)

loyalty—high commitment or faithfulness to a person or cause. (9)

M

Magnificat—the proclamation of Mary in response to God's blessing in the expected birth of the Savior, Jesus Christ (Luke 1:46-55). (4)

manner—pattern, model, way, habitual action; as in: pray in this manner. (13)

meditation—placing thoughts before your mind in order to move your heart toward God. (13)

meek—to have a controlled, gentle spirit even though the person has the power and authority to act. (12)

mercy—expression of sympathy, care and concern. (12)

Messiah—the Person prophesied in the Old Testament who was to become the Savior of the world. (2) (3)

metaphor—a language structure in which a word associated with one object is used with another object to make a comparison. (7) (14)

ministry—a service performed for the benefit of others for the purpose of bringing honor to God. (9)

miracles—events that supercede the laws of nature, performed by divine power and for a divine purpose; special exhibition of supernatural power; unusual events or phenomena which appear to violate natural laws but which reveal the omnipotence of God. (4) (7) (9) (15)

Mishnah—Jewish literature that interprets Mosaic Law. (11)

Mosaic Law—(Law) the laws given to Moses by God on Mount Sinai that defined religious, governmental and social life for the Israelites. The Law primarily refers to the Ten Commandments but would also include directions and principles recorded in Exodus and Leviticus. (11) (12)

Mount Hermon—a mountain at an elevation exceeding 9,000 feet north of the Sea of Galilee. It usually is snow covered all year and provides a steady stream of water to the Jordan River. (17)

mourners—people who show great sadness at the death of an individual. In Jesus' time they were often paid to stand close to the body while they loudly screamed and cried. (17)

mute—to be unable to speak; an older term was dumb as in a dumb animal. In the case of Zacharias, it seems he was also deaf. (4) (6) (17)

N

nature—internal quality of a person; one's character or attributes. (1)

O

oath—a vow or promise sworn as absolutely binding on the basis of some higher authority, such as God. (12)

omnipotent—all powerful, a characteristic exclusively related to God and His creation and control of the universe as well as the lives of individuals. (13)

omniscience—the ability to know everything at the same time; having all knowledge. Only God is omniscient. (5)

oral law—the traditions and practices added to Mosaic Law as rabbis interpreted and applied the laws to everyday life. These were then written more formally in the Mishnah. (11)

ordained—1) determined and directed to become according to God's will. 2) set apart or dedicated to God's service. (3)

orthodox—more conservative and traditional in the practice of religion; in accordance with historical laws and writings. (11)

P

Palestine—the land between the Mediterranean Sea and the Jordan River; in general, a reference to Israel and surrounding countries. Today it excludes Israel in continuing efforts to define a Palestinian homeland. (8)

parable—a story with two meanings, one that is natural and one that transcends to application in life or to spiritual truths. (14) (16)

paralytic—a person afflicted with an inability to move all or part of their limbs. (10)

Passover—an annual celebration of the exodus of the Israelites from Egypt during the time of Moses. (5)

perfect—complete, whole, completely integrated with no parts missing, without error. (12)

perish—to die or be destroyed; in an eternal sense, it is to be separated forever from the presence of God, a second or eternal death. (8)

persecution—hurting those who oppose you in belief, origin, religion, etc. (6)

persistence—continuing in effort, not giving up, keeping on. (13)

personality—the traits of an individual's social and emotional expressions that make him different from anyone else. (7)

perspective—viewing things according to their true nature or importance; Perceptions can be distorted from reality. Therefore we must have God's perspective. (4)

petition—asking God to meet your own needs or the needs of others. (13)

Pharisee—a member of a Jewish ruling sect that required strict observance of the law, both Old Testament and other Jewish writings such as the Talmud. They believed in the resurrection—that's why they were "fair, you see." (6) (8) (11)

poor in spirit—to be humble, selfless, not haughty, lowly in attitude. (12)

praise—to honor, adore, glorify by naming positive characteristics and accomplishments. (13)

prayer—consciously coming into God's presence as you seek to worship and know Him, and as you ask Him for your needs and the needs of others. (13)

preach—to proclaim God's Word, usually in a strong manner; to warn people of what God expects and coming judgment. (9)

pre-existence—living before; in relation to Christ, it refers to His life prior to birth on earth. (1)

Procurator—a governor assigned by Rome to a certain section of Israel to maintain control over the Jews. (8)

prophecy—the telling of events that will occur prior to their actually happening. Bible prophecy is sure to be fulfilled. (2) (3) (6)

pure in heart—internal truthfulness, integrity, without error. (12)

purpose—reason for action, goal to be accomplished, intention, plan. (2)

Q

quest—an adventurous journey to accomplish a specific purpose. (1)

R

rabbi—a teacher of the Old Testament Levitical law; a respected person, most knowledgeable of Old Testament writings and the Torah, who taught in Jewish synagogues. (5) (8)

Raca—a slur or derogatory remark indicating that a person is no good, without worth, a nobody. (12)

reconcile—to bring together in peace, to restore to a right relationship. (4)

redemption—buying back; ransom. God's redemption plan for mankind: forgiveness and salvation for those who receive Christ, every spiritual blessing, adoption as sons, holiness of people dedicated to Him. (2) (3)

refugee—a person who flees to a foreign country to escape danger or persecution. (5)

remnant—a small remainder. God preserved a remnant of the nation Israel to be His people and the family of Christ. (3)

repentance—a profound change of mind and heart that results in a change of behavior. (6)

revenge—retaliation, to get back at, to repay in the same way. (12)

righteousness—goodness, excellence of character and behavior; an act of God in which individuals are given right standing before God because of Christ's payment for their sins. (15)

S

Sabbath—"to cease from labor, to rest"; the seventh day, on which God rested from Creation; the day God blessed and made holy for Himself. (11)

Sadducee—a member of a ruling Jewish sect that did not adhere to the law as strictly as the Pharisees. They did not believe in the resurrection—that's why they were "sad, you see." (6) (11)

salvation—the saving of a person's soul from eternal death through belief and acceptance of Jesus as God's Son. (2) (8)

Sanhedrin—the governing council for political and spiritual life in Israel. Generally, it was controlled by the Pharisees and Sadducees. (8)

Satan—the devil (known as Lucifer, a fallen angel, that old serpent, the tempter, the deceiver, etc.,) who has been given limited power in the world, is an adversary to the purposes of God, and who will, one day, be confined eternally to hell. (7)

scarlet—red; the Bible presents Christ as the scarlet thread of redemption because we are saved through His blood. (2)

scribe—person who writes; in biblical times a scribe not only copied the Old Testament Scriptures, but interpreted and taught them in the synagogues. (10)

Sea of Galilee—a northern lake in Palestine connected by the Jordan River to the Dead Sea in the south. It is approximately 12 miles long and 6 miles wide. (17)

seek—to persist in looking for something. (13)

Sermon on the Mount—a popular name given to Jesus' message in Matthew 5, 6 and 7 in which He defined the behavior and attitudes of people in the Kingdom of God. (12)

silent years—the 400 years between the close of the Old Testament and the birth of Christ in the New Testament, in which no prophet spoke for God. (3)

simile—a language construction in which the similarities of an object are compared to a more abstract idea; similitude. (14)

similitude—an illustration in language in which the similarities of an object are compared to a more abstract idea. (12)

solitary—single, alone, quiet, contemplative. (1)

Son of Man—a name for Jesus Christ which refers to His being the promised Messiah, the son of Abraham and David's family; a name that identified Jesus as a Man in contrast to His divinity—the Son of God. (11)

sovereign—complete authoritative rule or dominion; in relation to God—omniscient (all-knowing), omnipotent (all-powerful) rule over the universe, including the lives of individuals. (13)

spiritual gifts—special talents and skills given to believers, such as preaching, teaching, helps, etc., for the work of ministry and assisting other saints. (7)

strategy—a plan of action with clearly defined objectives. (9)

synagogue—a Jewish meeting place for worship, prayer, teaching and community life. (9)

synoptic—being synonymous or similar as in Matthew, Mark, and Luke being the synoptic Gospels. (3)

T

Talitha, cumi—an Aramaic term meaning "Little girl, get up." (17)

tares—weeds and thorns, darnel which looks exactly like wheat until time for harvest. (16)

tax collector—a man who collects taxes for the government; in biblical times they worked for the Romans and were despised by the Jews both because of their dishonesty and because they were considered traitors. (10)

teach—to impart knowledge, to clearly explain and encourage someone to accept truth. (9)

temptation—1) the solicitation to do evil that occurs when an outward opportunity presents itself to a person who has an inward desire to sin. 2) a trying or testing that occurs as a normal course of life. (7) (13)

Tetrarch—ruler of the fourth country; a title for Herod the Tetrarch who ruled at the time Christ was born. (6)

tittle—the smallest character in the Hebrew alphabet, written above a letter much like an accent mark in English. (12)

transcendence—having meaning or application in a second, higher and more important way. For example, Aesop's Fables and the parables of Jesus have transcendent meaning. (14)

Trinity—the triune nature of God consisting of the Father, Son, and Holy Spirit—all three fully God but different expressions of the Godhead. (1)

trouble—condition of distress or discomfort, difficulty of life. (6)

trust—to place confidence in, to show faith, to utterly depend on, to believe strongly enough to lead to commitment. (10)

U

unique—special, without comparison, different from others. (1)

V

vain repetitions—words without thought or meaning that are repeated again and again, usually as a ritual of prayer. (13)

virgin—a person who has never had sexual relations. Jesus was born of the virgin Mary. (4)

virtue—essential essence of goodness; powerful or effective working. (17)

W

wayside—a path worn hard by walkers as they traveled through or around fields. (16)

word—a way to express meaning; the fundamental unit of communication. (1)

Word of God—Jesus Christ who came to earth to show mankind what God was like. Jesus is the living Word of God. The Bible is the written Word of God. (1)

worship—to attribute worth, to consider worthy in its highest or ultimate form. (8)

Z

zeal—enthusiasm, passion, commitment, jealousy toward an activity or person. (8)

Zealots—a Jewish religious sect that passionately wanted to free Israel from Roman rule and to restore the Old Testament law. (7)

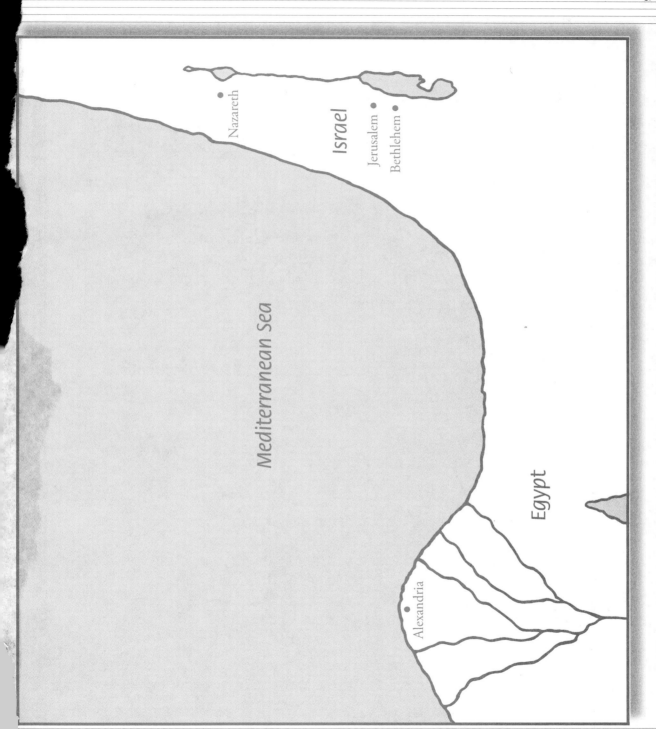

Nazareth

Israel

Jerusalem
Bethlehem

Mediterranean Sea

Egypt

Alexandria

Sidon

Damascus

MT. HERMON

Tyre

Phoenicia

Caesarea Philippi

Capernaum
Bethsaida
Magdala
Sea of Galilee
Cana
Nazareth
Tiberias
Gadara (Gerasenes)
Galilee
Nain
MT. TABOR

Mediterranean Sea

Jordan River

Decapolis

Caesarea

Samaria

Sychar

Perea

Bethel

Emmaus
Jericho
Bethabara

Jerusalem
Bethany
Bethlehem

Dead Sea

Gaza

Judea

Nazareth to Bethlehem—94 miles
Bethlehem to Jerusalem—6 miles
Jerusalem to Capernaum—96 miles

To Egypt—From Jerusalem 110 miles